MARLEE SILVA

MY TIDDA, MY SISTER

STORIES OF STRENGTH AND RESILIENCE FROM AUSTRALIA'S FIRST WOMEN

Artwork by Rachael Sarra

Hardie Grant
TRAVEL

For two of my nannas, Pearl and Alice.
Your battles and triumphs have taught me
what it truly means to be an Aboriginal woman.
I'm so proud to be yours,
I hope I am making you proud too.

ACKNOWLEDGEMENT

The majority of the work in this book was produced on the unceded lands of the Dharrawal and Gadigal peoples, where I work, live and have spent most of my life. As a Gamilaroi and Dunghutti girl, my people come from different nations to these, but this is where I feel at home. I am thankful to be able to thrive and create on these lands, and pay my respects every day to those who have come before me, our Elders present and those who will follow me in the future.

I acknowledge the unbroken connection between this continent and my people, which has lasted for over sixty thousand years. I draw strength from their resilience, woven into the fabric of the waterways and earth under my feet, and remember it always was and always will be Aboriginal land.

CONTENTS

PART I • AUNTIES PAST

PART II · TIDDAS PRESENT

PART III · YOU, THE FUTURE

SIS

noun

A person's sister. Their tidda, their backbone, the one who stands by them, who guides them, who wraps them up in love and asks for nothing but love in return.

FOREWORD

I am a Tidda, Sista, Sister, Sis, Sissy, Aunty (and a mother and a nan), and I could not help but smile with recognition as I read the stories that fill these pages of Marlee Silva's book *My Tidda, My Sister*. I could place myself or my mother or my nana into these stories and easily relate.

AS BLACKFELLAS, WE KNOW THESE STORIES, WE WILL SMILE AND NOD OUR HEADS, ACKNOWLEDGE OUR SHARED HISTORIES AND EXPERIENCES: THE GOOD AND THE BAD.

We also know the written stories on these pages will help our own, and will help the broader community of non-Indigenous peoples in an understanding of who we are as black women, from yesteryears, today and for all the tomorrows to come. That alone gives so much hope and strength, knowing our survival holds firm in the mindset of our younger First Nation's women, those in this very book.

My name is Leah Purcell, and I am a proud Goa Gunngari Wakka Wakka Murri woman, and it is a pleasure to be asked to write the foreword for Miss Marlee Silva's book *My Tidda, My Sister*.

When I was learning to use Instagram, and I was scrolling (chucking the terminology around here for effect because I have no idea, LOL) down, I came across Tiddas 4 Tiddas, and I immediately pressed 'follow'. This sort of site is what I have been about for many, many years: empowering Aboriginal women. Giving them a platform to raise their voices, to be heard. I have written and participated in books sharing stories of my own, and with other contemporary black women, and how we survive and navigate in today's world.

My first writing was my own story, covering three generations of Aboriginal women: my mum, Nana and my own life's stories in my play *Box the Pony*. Then came *Black Chicks Talking* – it started as a book that would become a bestseller. I was very proud of this because I had failed English! Black Chicks Talking became a play and then a documentary. I was thrilled when other community organisations came up with other uses for BCT and with their own versions of it: there was *More Black Chicks Talking* and *Murri Chicks Talkin' Up*, to name a few. This is why I write: to empower our Mob.

Being given the innate gift of storytelling, at times, can be a burden. But, I (we, all the other female Indigenous authors out there) understand this, it's our chosen path, a blessing from our ancestors to carry on culture as storytellers in modern times, and it can't be ignored. We shoulder the weight of writing about our families' and communities' past pains, to bring about understanding of our peoples' plight for others, giving us hope for a better future. We also have the responsibility to share all our achievements to empower our own talents, and to showcase our Mobs' talents to the world. It is our role.

IT IS OUR GIFT TO THOSE WHO FOLLOW. IT'S OUR WAY. IT IS OUR CULTURE, AND THAT'S JUST HOW IT GOES.

I wasn't aware of Marlee when I clicked 'follow' that day, but I thought, 'this is a young woman of my own heart'. Then, when talking to my partner, Bain (who's a big Rugby League fan), about how deadly I thought her Instagram platform is, he pointed out who her dad was, the silky, smooth fullback Rod Silva. Then Marlee approached me to be the subject of one of her podcasts, and I jumped at the opportunity to share my experiences and to encourage the next generation. I am in awe of this next generation: young, enthusiastic, intelligent on so many levels, and who continue to have the passion and drive to encourage, engage with and provide hope and strength to others; thas Blackfella way. It's who we are.

IT TAKES A GREAT DEAL OF COURAGE FOR ANYONE TO SHARE THEIR STORY, SO THANK YOU TO THESE WOMEN, BUT THEY WOULD NOT HAVE DONE THIS IF THEY DID NOT TRUST MARLEE, AND THAT IS A GIFT IN ITSELF, MARLEE!

These women wouldn't have opened up if Marlee wasn't open and honest in who she is and the journey she's been on, and through the pages of this book, you will witness this. So, thank you for your Dreaming, your honesty, bravery, skill and caring nature that makes for a nurturing platform – allowing others to give their Dreaming over to you as the sentinel of these gifts of story.

In this book, you will hear of personal challenges and triumphs, hardships and heartache, but all wrapped in hope and promise. I enjoyed reading this book; I was nodding my head in agreement; my eyes teared up in the shared experiences of their pain. There is lots of smiling at the funny personal situations and anecdotes, and when I finished the final page, I felt great pride!

To all the women in this book, I wish you well, but I know *you're all gonna be just fine, because you got ya tiddas watchin' ya backs!*

I believe this book will reach and speak in abundance to all who pick it up. These stories will never grow old, they will be shared by many of all races for many years to come.

TO BE CALLED SIS, SISSY, SISTER AND TIDDA IS HEART-WARMING, SOUL-ENRICHING; IT GIVES YOU A SENSE OF SECURITY AND A SENSE OF PRIDE THAT YOU BELONG, WHETHER YOU BE BLOOD OR NOT. SO, TO ALL THE TIDDAS, SISTERS READING THIS BOOK, NO MATTER WHERE YOU COME FROM, NO MATTER WHAT YOUR BACKGROUND OR HERITAGE IS, POWER TO YA!

Enjoy these Dreamings.
Peace

Leah Purcell
Actor/Writer/Director
Oombarra Productions

PREFACE

Picture this. You're in a foreign space, a new school, a bigger than expected university hall, the cafeteria at work on your first day at a new job, or a party you got dragged to and left behind at.

The room is filled to the brim with faces. There are familiar features, but an alien air to them. That one's got dance moves like another you know, but they're not quite to your beat. Yes, the movements look familiar, but you don't know their owners; they don't see you.

Empty air circles and weighs heavy all around, you grow impatient. Teetering on your tiptoes, you swallow and try to wet your dry throat, scan the clumps of trios and duos. You beg for a break in sound, a second to raise your voice and let them know your name.

But it doesn't look like its coming, and the knot at your belly button tugs you back down to flat feet. You turn inward and skulk across the room, towards a table, a corner, anywhere in the shadows. Yet you swear all eyes are on you.

Their daggers force your fingers to clasp at your clothes; pinch your clammy skin.

Something rises in your throat, a buzz in your ears so loud it muffles approaching footsteps.

And suddenly, the warmest phrase you know kisses the air: 'Hey sis'. Two syllables, two open arms. Ah, there you are.

Oh my sis, my sista, my deadly tidda girl.

On days that are long and life feels a whirl, it's you, a cuppa and your laugh that I need.

It's not a laugh, it's a cackle. One that carries up the street. One that pulls mine out too with a heave.

Koori, Murri, Noongar, Wiradjuri warrior princess. Doesn't matter if I've known you my whole life or little more than a breath. It's when we walk together that we walk tallest.

Black girl magic, that's what they call it, ay? Mystic, secret society, of nods and recognition, of 'you rights?' and a protective gaze.

I got your back, you've got mine. It's this bond that's kept all our mob together. An unspoken rule to ensure we survive.

Oh my sis, my sista, my deadly tidda girl.

ON DAYS THAT ARE LONG AND LIFE FEELS A WHIRL, IT IS YOU AND YOUR SACREDNESS. THAT'S ALL I NEED. IT'S US AND OUR BLACKNESS, THAT'LL ENSURE WE SUCCEED.

INTRODUCTION

Less than a thirty-minute drive (on a good day) south of the Sydney CBD sits a stretch of sand and sea as white and blue as most of the residents' skin and eyes. Cronulla, the pearl of the Sutherland Shire, is the only place I've ever known as home. My ancestors came from Britain and Germany on one side and, on the other, northern New South Wales, Gamilaroi and Dunghutti country in Moree and Kempsey; far quieter towns and far blacker than the one I've grown up in.

I've always known that I'm Aboriginal. But for a long time, I knew it in the same way that I knew I had a sister; that my postcode was 2228; that I was given the name Marlee Jade Silva on 15 September 1995 in a hospital room in Kogarah after fourteen hours of labour, and two weeks before my father would score the last try in the NRL Winfield Cup and win a premiership with the Canterbury–Bankstown Bulldogs.

FOR MOST OF MY CHILDHOOD, THE FACT THAT I HAVE FAIR-COLOURED SKIN AND EYES – THE PRODUCT OF MY MUM'S WHITENESS AND MY DAD'S BROWN SKIN – DIDN'T HAVE ANY EFFECT ON MY ABORIGINALITY. MY HERITAGE WAS A STURDY, UNQUESTIONABLE PART OF MY EXISTENCE.

I started my first year of secondary school at Port Hacking High in 2008, two years after the race riots that brought my hometown to the world's attention, and three weeks before the prime minister of the time, Kevin Rudd, made his National Apology address to the Stolen Generations.

Port Hacking High is a collection of red-brick buildings that have inhabited a corner block in the suburb of Miranda since 1959. It took the length of one song on morning radio to get from my childhood home to the school's main entrance along Kingsway, a road that stretches almost the entire breadth of the Sutherland Shire. And I quickly discovered that I was the only Aboriginal kid in my year.

BY MY SECOND WEEK OF YEAR 7, I'D FOUND THE COURAGE TO FORGE SOME FRIENDSHIPS WITH MY CLASSMATES. WHEN I GET NOSTALGIC WITH THE HIGH SCHOOL FRIENDS I STILL HAVE TODAY, WE CAN ALL RECALL VAGUE MEMORIES OF FIRST IMPRESSIONS: HOW WE BONDED OVER A SHARED LOVE OF HARRY POTTER OR PLAYFULLY ARGUED OVER WHOSE FAVOURITE FOOTY TEAM WAS BETTER.

There's only one of these encounters, though, that I remember in intricate detail, almost word for word. One girl – blonde, tall, pale skin, not unlike many of my other friends – asked a question that will remain with me for the rest of my life.

We struck up a conversation after a science class when she'd called someone else's name and I'd misheard it as my own. She seemed like a very suitable friend choice, although, admittedly, anyone who was willing to talk to me at this point was appealing.

At the end of the first week when we became friends, the final bell of the day rang at 3.05pm. The sky opened with a summer afternoon storm. It was a torrential downpour with blasts of thunder so loud it deafened the squeals of hundreds of schoolkids as they ran or skipped or danced through it. My new friend and I headed towards the bus bay and said goodbye to the comfort of dry uniforms. Then we were running and giggling towards the gate, happily welcoming fat water drops on our cheeks.

As we got to the gate, I went to say what would have been an awkward but sincere *Seeyalater! Add me on MySpace!*-kind-of farewell, when I was stopped by a deep voice calling out my name. I peered up to find a man waiting at the exit.

Wrinkling a smile in my direction, he stood there in his flannelette shorts, white with navy pinstripes, a grey shirt with a dried coffee stain in the centre, with stubble that a younger me might have called a 'scratchy beard' and heavy bags under his eyes – all perfectly paired with bright-blue, shin-high gumboots.

The rain danced around his four-person umbrella, but I didn't dare approach it. My face burnt and my shoulders hunched; I clenched my fists around my bag straps and turned my attention to the asphalt below.

It was my dad. He called out to me again, only this time he didn't say Marlee, but screamed 'Mooky!' (a nickname nobody else had used since I was five) and waved with excitement as I mistakenly made eye contact.

I hoped with all my might that my new friend hadn't realised he was addressing me, as I turned to quickly say goodbye to her and moved in the vague direction of Dad. Weaving through the sea of uniforms and regulation black-leather shoes, I made it to the passenger door of our white Honda Civic without indicating any connection to him.

IN HINDSIGHT, IT WAS VERY KIND OF HIM TO BRAVE THE RAIN TO MAKE SURE I DIDN'T GET WET.

But at the time I was convinced my father was committed to totally destroying my chances of developing a social life. After refusing to talk to him on the drive home, I cooled down and refocused my energy on crossing all of my appendages throughout the weekend, hoping that anyone who witnessed my mortified moment would have completely forgotten about it before rollcall on Monday.

However, in second period on Monday I had science with my new friend again. Her blonde side ponytail sat at the desk ahead of me, and as our teacher left the room to photocopy worksheets, she swung it around to ask the dreaded question.

'Who was that who picked you up on Friday? In the gumboots?'

I felt my face blush and my heart sink all over again. I remember attempting to laugh it off it, as I admitted the gumbooted man in question was my dad. But while I'd been so sure that she'd laugh at me or embarrass me further, she surprised me with a response I could never have imagined.

'Is he your stepdad? Or your *real* dad?'

At first, I figured she was hoping to spare me from biological relation to his shamelessness, laughing through the discomfort once more. 'Um, yeah, he's my real dad.'

I can still see the way she tilted her head and squinted her eyes slightly, confused, before she expressed the single most defining question of my life: 'Why is your dad *black*?'

So in 2008 I had someone paint colour onto my world for the very first time.

Soon after I explained to her that we are Aboriginal, to which she responded, stunning me once more, 'No way! I've never met an Aboriginal before!'

Then, it felt as though I'd been found out by my whole school, and I was instantly confronted with an onslaught of questions and reactions that I was in no way prepared for.

'Do you believe in the Dreamtime?'

'Like, how much Aboriginal are you though? One quarter? A sixteenth?'

I was ashamed when I couldn't come up with the right answers and very quickly, I became obsessed with building myself into a spokesperson of sorts for Aboriginal Australia, to counter my white friends and even whiter school environment. I collected every story I could from my family, read every bit of history I could find, and emerged as someone who was bitter with the injustices we had faced and continue to, but also determined to be a leader and a positive representation of my people.

A FEW YEARS LATER, MY CONFIDENCE IN WHO I WAS STRENGTHENED.

But frustration with other people's misunderstandings, and my teenage angst in general, only grew. By this time, the people who existed in my school context had got all their burning questions and wonderings out of their systems, with mostly innocent motives, but the outside world wasn't done with me yet, and the strain on my emotions began to show.

One day, in response to someone telling me I wasn't *really* Aboriginal (not for the first time) because of my fair skin, I broke down. In amongst our daily ritual of family catch-ups over dinner, tears dampened my lasagna as I succumbed to the pain of that question over my identity. I'd been fighting so hard, but nothing seemed to be changing. I remember the sadness bubbling in my gut, rising as fury and erupting with an exclamation of, 'I *hate* white people.' I felt Mum wince, Dad told me to watch my mouth and remember I am the product of two cultures, but I just spat back at them that I wished I wasn't.

Dad called me to the kitchen the morning after my meltdown and I found him at our bench in front of two ceramic mugs and a carton of milk.

'Come watch this.' He gestured at me to look into the mugs: they were both filled halfway with black coffee. His callused hands picked up the milk and poured an inch of it into one of the cups, turning its contents a creamy brown.

'Tell me what you're looking at.' I shrugged, but he urged me on. 'They're cups of coffee, right?'

'Well, yeah, I guess so ... '

'No. No guessing. No doubt. They're coffee. Both of them. It's what they've always been and what they'll always be. This one' – he gestured to the lighter-coloured liquid – 'is no less coffee than the other. It doesn't matter how much milk you add: they'll never **not** be coffee.'

I still carry that image with me today, as a shield. One which brushes off brows that furrow when I wear a t-shirt with my flag on it to a music festival; or eyes that pop when someone spots the tattoo on the back of my ankle and is greeted with the knowledge that the *yurrandaali*, or tree goanna, is my family totem; or even ponders out loud that if my claimed race is true, does this mean I receive government handouts for everything?

Never not coffee, never not coffee, I think over and over, but no protection is completely indestructible.

DURING THOSE TEENAGE YEARS, I DISCOVERED ANOTHER SHIELD AND SOURCE OF STRENGTH TOO: THE SISTERHOOD. THE FIRST TIME I FELT ITS POWER, I MUST'VE BEEN JUST FIFTEEN. I WAS SENT ON A CAMP FOR YOUNG INDIGENOUS LEADERS ON THE GOLD COAST FOR A WEEK.

It was the first time I flew on a plane without my parents and when I arrived, I'd find I was the youngest of the one hundred or so other high school students in attendance.

At the time, I'd not quite graduated from crop tops to proper underwire bras, I had a mouth full of metal, a side fringe and (in my opinion) I had an affliction for sucking at making new friends. In a word, I'd describe fifteen-year-old Marlee as: awkward.

We're all a bit awkward at one point during our teenage years. Overall, adolescence is an inherently awkward process, really. I mean, think about it, overnight you're practically stuffed into this bizarre new body, covered in lumps and bumps you've never had before, and forced to navigate weird new experiences and feelings without a map.

Almost like a caterpillar hiding in a cocoon, before you've had the time to build your wings and get the hell out of there, you go through this phase where you kind of turn to mush and get left feeling hyper vulnerable. During that time, you manage to trick yourself into thinking you're the only one going through it all, when in reality you're surrounded by other chrysalis busting to get to the relief on the other side of it, just like you.

That time on the Gold Coast was peak fragility for me. Growing up an Aboriginal female – in an almost exclusively white area of Sydney – made for a few sweet opportunities for my peers who felt crappy about themselves to find reason to … kick my cocoon, so to speak.

I got to this leadership camp at a point in my life where things like going up to pay for something at my corner store and having to speak to the worker on the other side of the counter made me squirm and feel short of breath. So you can imagine the state I was in when I was then shoved into a room full of complete strangers, most of whom were two years older than I was, and forced to introduce myself.

I remember the first day of the camp pretty clearly. It was February in Queensland, a wet, sticky heat sat in the air. Everyone was sweating, so at least that element of my nerves wasn't noticeable.

ONCE WE ALL ARRIVED, GETTING OUT OF OUR RESPECTIVE CABS AND BUSES, THERE WAS A BUNCH OF EAGER STAFF IN WHITE POLO SHIRTS, LIKE THE ONES WE'D SOON HAVE TO ADORN OURSELVES, WAITING OUTSIDE THE VENUE READY TO GREET US.

Typical blackfulla style, a lot of us were late and the intended timing wasn't going to plan, so thankfully for me, there was no time for intros or awkward silences and we were herded straight through to a room for registration. I think it must've been a dressing room, or at least it felt like a dressing room in a footy shed, in my memory. What stands out is the uncomfortable ground we sat on, it was that rubber asphalt you only find on running tracks and in footy sheds. I remember the rather pathetic, lone fan in the corner of the room too, and how it did little to relieve us as we were told to sit and wait to be addressed about the rules of the camp and the plans for the rest of the day.

The waiting seemed to stretch on and on, so of course, being a room full of kids, we quickly got restless. What began as bubbling murmurs, quickly erupted into loud conversations and cackling laughter. In my fear and shyness, my heart sank as it seemed like everyone already knew each other, like they all had already formed their groups within fifteen minutes of being together and I, as per usual, had missed the boat.

When I'd been in situations like this before I'd usually try embarrassingly hard to get someone's attention and force them to speak to me by doing this creepy thing, where I'd stand a little too close to groups of people, but not quite close enough to actually look like I was hanging out with them, and eavesdrop on their conversations. Not because I was interested in what they were saying necessarily, but because I'd look for a point in their topics to chime in.

That point never seemed to come and instead, in my desperation, I'd end up just laughing loudly whenever the group did, whilst making uncomfortable eye contact with them, which would result in all present realising I was there and turning to stare at me. It would occasionally get a pity recognition and 'what's your name?', but it wasn't pretty, nor sustainable for new friendship prospects.

But this day, as I scanned the little cross-legged circles around me getting prepared to listen in on one of their conversations, I was shocked to feel a pair of girls nearby turn towards me. I couldn't tell you their names, but I remember one of them had freckles across her cheeks and a big smile, and the other wore electric blue nail polish, painted with impressive precision. They were obviously older, more confident, without the same slightly hunched posture I held, and I was chuffed as they smiled at me and waved me over. I momentarily forgot how to move my legs, but eventually got up and hurried to sit beside them.

'Hey sis, where'd you get that?' She, the one with the freckles, pointed at the necklace dangling at my chest, it was a dog tag on a chain, printed with the Aboriginal flag and words below it that read: *KOORI PRIDE*.

'Um, Yabun, you know the Survival Day festival in Sydney?' We all remember ourselves in the worst light, but I'm sure I couldn't make eye contact with her in saying that.

'OH YEAH THAT'S DEADLY, I NEED ONE. IS THAT WHERE YOU'RE FROM SIS? SYDNEY? WHO'S YA MOB DOWN THERE?'

WHAT PROCEEDED FROM HERE IS THE SAME CONVERSATION I'VE HAD WITH EVERY ABORIGINAL PERSON I'VE EVER MET SINCE. IT'S ONE OF THE MOST BEAUTIFUL THINGS ABOUT OUR CULTURE, AND THAT DAY, IT TAUGHT ME THE POWER WE HAVE IN OUR STRENGTH AS ONE MOB, ONE FAMILY.

If you're not Indigenous you might not have seen this before, but all my tiddas out there will know it for sure. You see, when blackfullas meet, it's our instinct to first find out how we're connected to each other. Whether it's through blood, through the country we're from or through people we know in common, we are interested first and foremost in what brings us together, and you best believe we always find a link.

I'll show you how it works in my case. When I meet a brother or sister anytime, anywhere, I can almost guarantee they'll say, 'What's your name? Who's ya mob? Where you from?'

And I'll say, 'I'm Marlee Silva, my mob's Gamilaroi – Frenchs from Moree, and Dunghutti – Silvas from Kempsey.'

And they'll think for a second before they say, 'Who's Janine French to you?'

And I'll say, 'She's my cousin.'

And they'll say, 'I used to work with Janine. How is she? Still up in Moree? Tell her I said hello.'

Or they'll say, 'Kempsey Silvas? Who are your grandparents?'

And I'll say, 'My pop was Batman Silva.'

And their eyes will widen and they'll stand back, getting a better look at me before saying, 'Aye, no way! We're related,' then they'll call someone else over and say, pointing at me,

'Look 'ere, meet my cousin Marlee. Marlee Silva, Kempsey Silvas, Batman's granddaughter, remember Batman?'

EVERY TIME I GET TO EXPERIENCE THIS BEAUTIFUL EXCHANGE, JUST LIKE THAT FIRST TIME, WHEN I WAS FIFTEEN, NO MATTER THE CONTEXT, I COME AWAY FROM THE MOMENT FEELING INSTANTLY BETTER. MORE AT EASE, MORE LIKE I'M WHERE I'M SUPPOSED TO BE – WHERE I BELONG.

You've probably picked up that I was a bit of a loner as a teen, and I was terribly lonely too. I spent a lot of time at school, feeling that nobody understood me or really knew me at all. I realise in hindsight, it was mostly because I *was* an odd one out. I was the only Aboriginal kid in my year, one of five identifying kids in my school (one of whom was my little sister) and my many cousins and other friends I made at camps like the one on the Gold Coast, that I loved and yearned to be around so much, lived so far away from me.

We, as Aboriginal and Torres Strait Islander people, stand together, as one, supportive, loving network of people who, for the most part, care for and treat each other like family.

PARTICULARLY OUR WOMEN ARE DEDICATED TO LIFTING EACH OTHER UP AND ACTING AS EACH OTHER'S BIGGEST CHEERLEADERS AND FANS, IN WAYS THAT I RARELY SEE HAPPEN WITH NON-INDIGENOUS WOMEN AND GIRLS.

The levels of jealousy and the 'love to hate' mentality, although not completely absent for Aboriginal women, is so much less prevalent in our circles, with our tiddas. This comes back to our history, our survival over eighty thousand years, which was enabled and led by our matriarchs. Our women have always been the ones who've held us together, in order for us to not just survive, but to thrive.

It's such a huge part of what inspired me to create Tiddas 4 Tiddas in November of 2018. The enormous power and inspiration of the women around me, the women I call my Aunties and my sisters, that seemed to be going by unnoticed outside of our circles. I needed a place to shout our brilliance to the heavens, because the strength I get from my tiddas is what enables my own. There are lessons in the 'tidda-hood' that all those who identify as female, regardless of race, religion and skin colour, can learn from, be inspired by and come to celebrate. So, that's how I've landed here, in the first pages of this book.

My Tidda, My Sister will only scratch the surface of the experiences of some of our most influential and educational Aunties and tiddas, from the past and present, before launching into the hopes and possibilities of all of you, for the future. Dive into this with an open mind and an open heart.

MY BEAUTIFUL BLACK SISTERS, I HOPE YOU SEE YOURSELF AND YOUR POTENTIAL TO DO ANYTHING AND EVERYTHING IN THESE PAGES – YOU HAVE THE POWER THESE WOMEN EXEMPLIFY COURSING THROUGH YOUR VEINS.

My non-Indigenous sisters, be ready to be challenged, to learn, to grow, and all of us together will build a brighter tomorrow.

Marlee Silva

PART I

AUNTIES PAST

Your colourless skin, soft as velvet shine.

What can I tell you, daughter of mine?

I could tell you of heartbreak, hatred blind,

but instead, I'll tell you of bravery, victory and pride –

now, lives of black and white entwine –

and men and women alike combine.

The fight is not over, but the future is bright –

it is yours in due time.

This I would tell you – oh daughter of mine.

A RESPONSE TO AUNTY OODGEROO NOONUCCAL'S POEM, 'SON OF MINE'.

AUNTY

noun

A female leader. A source of guidance, a person who holds great wisdom, who should be shown the utmost respect; and be served a cup of tea and biscuits upon arrival anywhere.

'TRY NOT
TO GIVE UP'

VIOLET PEARL FRENCH
GAMILAROI

In February of 1918, in Gulargambone, New South Wales (Wailwan country) on the banks of the Castlereagh River, my great-grandmother Violet Pearl Groves was born.

At this time, Australia was emerging a different country on the other side of World War I. Gallipoli birthed the ANZAC spirit and held a mirror up to the colony. Stepping out from under the shadow of the British crown, what did it mean to be an Australian? Back then – and perhaps even today – it was fair to say, to be accepted as an 'Aussie', you had to be white.

This was at a time when my people were still counted with the native plants and animals in the census. It's a time when we were living mostly on missions, places we'd been herded onto like cattle, away from our homelands. Where a 'Protector of Aborigines' governed us, held the power to permit or deny us from leaving the mission, restricted the rations we survived off, policed our practice of culture and language, and perpetrated the theft of our children.

I imagine that the day on which Violet took her first breath was still. Not the kind of still that is ominous or unsettling, but a peaceful still. The usually gurgling river would be silent, the leaves wouldn't rustle, a wind would barely blow. All would stop to watch.

HER MUMS WOULD'VE HOVERED AROUND HER, CLEANING HER UP, SINGING TO HER. THEIR LOVE WOULD PROVE TO BE SO POWERFUL THAT IT COVERED AND SHIELDED HER FOR HER WHOLE NINETY YEARS OF LIFE.

You see, my Nanny Pearl, despite the state of the Australia that she lived and grew up in, travelled through life with unshakeable positivity, and kindness was the basis for her every move.

In the decades following her birth and childhood beside that watching river, Nan Pearl would go on to marry a Gamilaroi man named James and become Violet Pearl French. The two would move to Moree and there raise around a dozen children. The number's vague because, while we know they had eleven biological children of their own, my great nan and pop had a habit of taking in other young ones who needed a home.

For ten years the large family lived in little more than a tin humpy on a dried-up riverbed. It wouldn't have looked like much to those on the outside, but I'm certain it was full of love. Pop worked as a shearer and Nan cleaned houses. It was said she'd walk the five or so kilometres into town from the mission every day, more often than not with a few kids hanging off her.

When Nan Pearl passed away in her nineties, she had lived to see 242 grandchildren, great-grandchildren and great-great-grandchildren be born. This meant she was in high demand, and I didn't get to spend as much time with her growing up as I would've liked. Despite that, I have no doubt that her story and her leadership as our family's unshakeable matriarch has had a greater impact on me, who I am now and who I want to be, than anyone else.

TO ME, NAN PEARL EXEMPLIFIES RESILIENCE.

There's this old newspaper clipping we have that features her. It was published in the *Moree Champion* in 1986, the year she was named both Senior Citizen and Aboriginal Elder of the year.

In it she talks about the hard times: 'We had no glass windows or fans or electricity. I remember having to make a fire and walking for miles with an old kerosene can on a yoke for water.'

I don't really remember what her voice sounded like or how she spoke, but the same woman who delivered Meals on Wheels to the elderly well into her eighties would not have said this with bitterness.

Dad says she was matter of fact and, despite the little they did have, she always found enough to give more to others. She gave love, cups of tea, words of wisdom, a shoulder to cry on, a place to sleep and so much more, to so many.

In that same *Moree Champion* article, Nan mentions all the times they were bothered by police on the mission, how they had to be so careful around them, how they had to ask permission to get more tin and extend the humpy they'd built.

I've also heard a story from one of my uncles about a time Nan needed urgent medical attention. The mission master had called an ambulance, but it refused to come onto the mission. Nan couldn't walk, so Pop scooped her up and ran her through the mission, across the riverbed, to the ambulance instead.

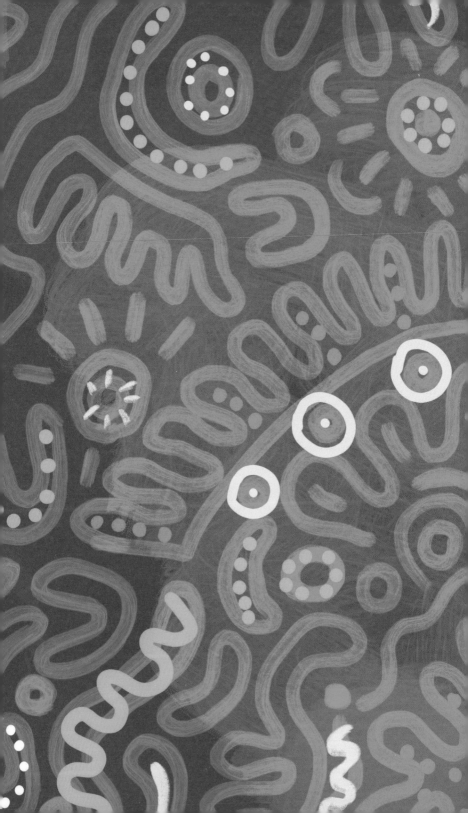

That story never gets easier to hear. Nan was tiny, Pop was nearly seven feet tall. I can see him, his long black legs and skinny ankles moving as fast as they could down the riverbed, brown dust rising in the air behind him. His calloused shearer's hands full, clinging onto his whole world. The kids left behind, not knowing what was going on. No doctor there to tell them what was happening, that their mum was going to be okay. All that fear, all that uncertainty and, ultimately, the trauma of a miscarriage, would weigh on each of them, purely as a result of the colour of their skin.

WHEN ASKED HOW SHE MADE IT THROUGH ALL THE TOUGH TIMES, NAN SAID, 'YOU CAN'T KEEP LOOKING BACK, WE MUST ALWAYS ONLY LOOK FORWARD.' LOOK TO TOMORROW, LOOK TO THE PATH SHE CARVED FOR US AND FIGURE OUT HOW WE WOULD CONTINUE PAVING IT FOR THE NEXT.

SHE HAD A MOTTO THAT SHE STOOD BY, TOO: 'TRY NOT TO GIVE UP.'

Nan Pearl first passed the motto on to her daughter Alice, my grandmother, my dad's mum. A similarly stoic, hardworking, resilient black woman. That attitude helped Nan Alice find the strength and resilience to turn up to high school every day, regardless of the obstacles she faced there. She was the only Aboriginal student at the time and every day she would face an onslaught of racial slurs and quite often experience disgusting bullying acts, like peers spitting on her.

Despite it all, with 'try not to give up' echoing in her mind, not only did she become the first Aboriginal graduate from her high school, but she is also the first female Aboriginal to graduate with a Bachelor of Social Work at the University of Sydney, which, by the way, she attained whilst raising five children in a housing commission place in Western Sydney.

Unfortunately Nan Pearl, now in her later years of life, has been diagnosed with dementia and there will be memories and stories that will be lost with her one day.

A few years back, when the disease was in its earliest stages, I was with Nan Pearl at a community event and felt devastated to see how the dementia was already affecting her. She got confused and anxious really easily, kept asking me my name too. But one thing that seemed unscathed were the memories of her achievements.

MORE THAN ONCE SHE LEANED OVER TO ME, PLACING HER COOL, SLENDER FINGERS ON MY ARM AND WHISPERED WITH A SMIRK, 'DO YOU KNOW I WAS THE FIRST ABORIGINAL WOMAN TO GRADUATE FROM SYDNEY UNI?'

When you're a trailblazer out on the frontlines, doing it so others can follow, I guess even as your mind starts to lose its way, your bones and your breath never forget the path you've forged.

My Nan Alice's second youngest child was born in 1967, my dad Rodney. He was one of the first blackfullas to be counted as an Australian citizen, in that same year that the referendum was passed his blood was already pumping with my nan's motto.

For my dad, his siblings and his mum, aside from the pressures of being poor and black in a still discriminatory Australia, they were forced to navigate another obstacle: my Poppy Silva's alcoholism. Dad's only started telling us about it in the last couple of years, but Pop got violent on the drink. He'd work long hours as a crane driver, and on pay day drink all his money, before coming home and taking out the pain inside of him on his wife and children.

Nan Alice and Dad refused to ever consider giving up during this period. Dad said it taught him how to overcome anything, and it showed him the kind of father he didn't want to be and also highlighted the sheer strength of his mother. His favourite childhood memories are all from school holidays spent with Nan Pearl up in Moree, with all his cousins, surrounded by love, distracted from the turmoil at home.

Overall, it is the resilience passed down through his maternal lineage that saw Dad, who was nicknamed 'Rocket Rod', escape the poverty of his upbringing and live a fourteen-year-long career as a professional NRL player. And now, my sister and I have had the best possible life, because of him and my mum's hard work.

'TRY NOT TO GIVE UP' IS MY GREAT-GRANDMOTHER'S LEGACY. I HEAR IT AS A MESSAGE ON LOOP, WHISPERED OVER AND OVER IN MY EARS ON THE DAYS WHEN LIFE SEEMS A LITTLE TOO HARD. IT SOUNDS SO SIMPLE, BUT ITS REFLECTIVE OF AN INHERENT BELIEF IN THE FACT THAT YOU HAVE THE POWER TO DETERMINE YOUR FUTURE.

You might be dealt a rough hand or be forced to face injustice, but it's your choice what you do with it. Will you let it knock you down? Or will you just try not to give up and turn it into a fire in your belly? A purpose? A reason to keep fighting to make a better tomorrow for you and those you care about?

The stories of my grandmothers are more important to me than anything else. They are an infinite source of education, inspiration, guidance and hope. I'm so proud of my family. So proud of the defiance they've shown over decades, their success against the odds. They constantly remind me the truth about the limits of my capabilities – that there are none.

One thing my Nan Pearl taught me is that we, as human beings, have the potential to do so much more than we think. We have hands that can build tin humpies filled with love, where social workers and academics and sportsmen and Aboriginal leaders can be raised. We have voices that can carry through generations, that can determine the successes of our children and grandchildren.

'ALL WE NEED TO DO IS STAND TALL, STICK OUT OUR CHESTS AND LET THE WORLD HEAR US ...

LET'S TALK ABOUT
MENTAL HEALTH

Trigger warning: Discussion of suicide

WE ARE OFTEN TOLD ABOUT THE INTER-GENERATIONAL TRAUMA WOVEN INTO OUR DNA, BUT NEVER FORGET ABOUT THE RESILIENCE AND STRENGTH IN THERE TOO.

Death is often traumatic and devastating, but when it comes in the form of suicide, it is pain of a far deeper level. It's the type of pain that raises questions that keep you up at night; the type that makes you angry; the type that leaves you wanting to fight for change so nobody else ever feels like that's their only choice, ever again; and devastatingly, it's a type of pain Aboriginal and Torres Strait Islander communities know better than most.

The Aboriginal youth suicide rate is the second highest of any country in the world. I am no expert, I've not studied psychology or anything of the sort – I am merely a Gamilaroi and Dunghutti woman, who sees this crisis in reality.

When we consider the research that says we're five times more likely to take our own lives than our non-Indigenous counterparts, to my black brothers and sisters and I, these facts and figures have names and faces.

WE KNOW OF THE FAMILIES THAT HAVE EMPTY CHAIRS AT THE DINNER TABLE, NEVER TO BE FILLED AGAIN. WE'VE SEEN AND FELT THE HOLLOWNESS THAT COMES WITH THESE STATISTICS.

The horrible truth is, I don't know a single Aboriginal person in my life that has not been affected by suicide. How has it come to this?

Prior to invasion, the concept of suicide was not known to Aboriginal people; it was not part of our culture or our way of living. A senate enquiry into the decimating impact of this issue has found that suicides of Aboriginal and Torres Strait Islander peoples are often linked to 'despair caused by the history of dispossession combined with the social and economic conditions in which Aboriginal and Torres Strait Islander peoples live'.

It is undeniable that our battle with mental ill health and suicide is directly linked to colonisation. But what can we as Australians, both black and white, do to help change it now? That is a huge and complex question I'm not qualified to answer, but I think each day people can and must start with finding better ways to come together, build a culture of utilising professional help and take the time every day to show those around us that we support and care about each other's wellbeing.

Monique Rosas, an Aboriginal mother and photographer from the Atherton Tablelands, opened up about her journey to acceptance around the struggles she's had with her mental health management, her decision to speak to a professional and how it made all the difference.

Monique is unashamed to talk about the trauma she faced within her family growing up and how the resulting struggle to connect to her culture, identity and sense of self contributed to her mental health issues later in life. She didn't always feel so okay with being open about it, though. For a long time, when the turmoil occurring inside of her would emerge through aggressive or seemingly illogical reactions to stressful situations, people would call her 'crazy'. Unfortunately she started to believe them and fell deeper inside herself, feeling lost and a little hopeless.

But when she fell pregnant with her first child, the excitement and weight of the big change that was about to occur helped her shed the shame and fear. It was then she first saw a psychologist, a decision she now sees as one of the best she's ever made.

'She told me I wasn't crazy. She made me feel like I was okay and I was normal, I just had generalised anxiety.'

Not only did this professional help Monique to see that it was okay to not feel okay, she also offered coping mechanisms to manage her relationship with herself and others. Now, Monique says she and her partner are working better to not sweat the small stuff in life, and are able to step back and look at the bigger picture, thanks to the work they've done together with her psychologist.

Monique is thriving with her three children and partner, working every day to grow more and more as a proud Aboriginal woman, and committed to helping other blackfullas know their beauty and expand the reach of their businesses through her photography work.

'I would recommend it to everyone. It's good to talk to someone that's not family or a friend too because you can say anything and everything you're feeling and thinking.'

Mental health issues are not something that can be cured like the common cold. For most of us who deal with it, it will never go away completely. But it doesn't have to control your life, and one of the ways to reduce its impact is through a professional such as a psychologist, counsellor or psychiatrist. They can help you understand what's going on, recognise what triggers your dark feelings or emotions, and build coping and management mechanisms that work best for you.

If you are feeling like you're in a dark place, please remember how hard our ancestors fought for you to exist; you are their wildest dreams and every breath you take is one we take together. You matter and there's more love for you than you could ever know.

If you need help or want to read more on how you can help others, consider these options:

- If it is an emergency and you or someone around you feels your life is in immediate danger, call emergency services on **000**.
- **Lifeline** is a not-for-profit organisation that provides free, 24-hour Telephone Crisis Support service in Australia, it can be called at any time on **13 14 11**.
- Organisations like **Headspace** and **Beyond Blue** have extensive resources to better understand mental health. Your options for seeking health and how to help out a friend you think might be having a tough time can all be accessed online or via an app.
- **ACCHOs** or Aboriginal Community Controlled Health Organisations, like your local Aboriginal Medical Centre, are a great first stop to figure out culturally safe options for mob in your local area. Any GP can provide options and information too.

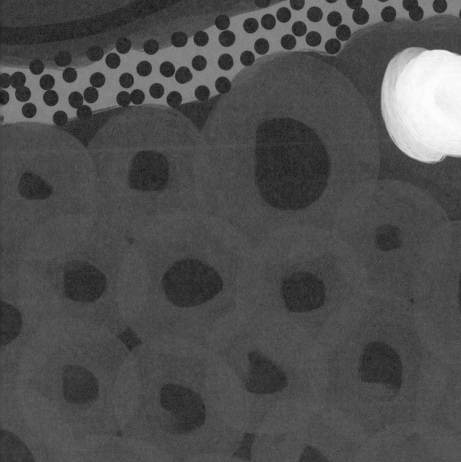

'BE INSPIRED TO KEEP GOING NO MATTER WHAT'

In memory of
LAVINA PIETENS
(nee Cunningham)
BIRIPI

Picture this: it's 1979 and your son invites you down to the beautiful coastal town of Forster, New South Wales, to join him where he is holidaying. You grew up visiting your grandmother there and now, thirty-five years later, you are excited to go back with your mum and your husband, to relive some of the memories from that time, and see how the place has changed.

You plan to stay in the same motel as your son, and when you arrive, you go to the front office to book a room and check in. As you approach the person at the front desk, you feel a far too familiar sense of dread, as the woman's eyes scan and dissect you and your mother's black skin. Your fears surge when you ask for a room for three and are told there's none available.

Your suspicions are confirmed when you meet the owner of the motel in the carpark shortly afterwards, and are told what the receptionist has told you is untrue. There are plenty of rooms available, and it takes the owner's authority to override the actions of the receptionist and find you a place to stay.

This is what happened to Biripi woman Lavina Pietens (nee Cunningham). Furious about how little things had change for her people over the years, she wrote to *The Sydney Morning Herald* newspaper in 1979 in the hopes of relating her disgust and disappointment to the broader public. Here's a snippet of the powerful words she wrote, titling it 'Discrimination':

'As a child, thirty-five years ago, every Xmas I visited my grandmother who lived at Forster. The scene was sand hills and bush. The sound of many wild birds. The most activity was the main street where my grandmother lived.

A night out was walking to the surf or around the lakes. A night at the picture show, where one side of the theatre was for the coloured people and the other side was for the whites. One had to pay admission to the swimming pool but the Aboriginal people were not allowed in to swim. This was the first time I felt the hurt of being a different colour …

The scenery has changed after all these years. Large flats everywhere, beautiful homes. No land, hills and lovely bush – no sounds of native birds, it is just like Manly. But the people have not changed after all these years, the discrimination is still there. I have lived a good life. My mother is a religious woman and raised us the same, with education and self-respect, but what chances does one have with these crook[s].

I am going overseas to represent my country in my sport and am very proud as I always have tried to achieve this goal. But then to be treated like this by Australians – it hurts. I thank the owner of the flats, he is one and I know there are other white Australians, many of my friends who take me as I am with no colour barrier.

I WILL BE DOING MY BEST WHEN AWAY FOR AUSTRALIA, AS I AM PROUD TO BE AN AUSTRALIAN ABORIGINAL AND HOPE TO PROVE, GIVEN THE CHANCE, AND BEING TREATED EQUAL, WE CAN LIVE IN HARMONY AS WE ARE ALL THE SAME UNDER THE COLOUR OF OUR SKIN.

There is good and bad in all races, but it is always enhanced more when one is coloured.'

I watched Lavina tell the story of this incident via a video her granddaughters sent me. She was eating a mango on the back porch of her Forrest Beach home in Queensland, and as she spoke in response to a question about what she thought was the best thing about being a blackfulla, I began to understand why she looked up, scoffed and answered, 'What is anything good about being Aboriginal?'

Where Lavina mentions in the letter about representing Australia, she's referencing her success in the sport of tenpin bowling. She was a competitive bowler most of her life as a result of what she described as practice and practice to perfection, and she landed a spot on the Australian national tenpin bowling team. This success saw her travel the world competing and becoming the first Aboriginal woman to partake in a tenpin bowling world cup.

We are unfortunately familiar with this trope of Aboriginal athletes who are revered for their talent, skills and achievements, but still experience discrimination off the field or when they choose to speak up. It's similar to the way that a smoking ceremony, an acknowledgement of country or even an Aboriginal dance troupe at an opening ceremony, or a sporting event on the world stage, are often seen as an entertaining spectacle for the audience, rather than as a genuine act of respect and acknowledgement of our people and culture. This tokenism even extends to some of our greatest athletes, who have much higher and heavier expectations placed upon them than their non-Indigenous peers, leaving them vulnerable to racism if they dare step out of their box.

We saw the outrage that came with Olympic runner Cathy Freeman's choice to do her victory lap in 2000 with both the Australian and Aboriginal flags draped over her shoulders. It's in the stories told by Olympic champion Nova Peris about being called an 'n-word' by a fellow Australian athlete. There are more recent examples, like the tirade of Australian media and booing spectators against AFL star Adam Goodes in the final years of his career. Similarly, in the sport of rugby league, stars like Latrell Mitchell and Cody Walker have been vilified for choosing not to sing the Australian national anthem.

It seems our sports stars are allowed to be black only when it results in a win on the field.

'ALWAYS LOVE AND SUPPORT ONE ANOTHER. LOVE GOES A LONG WAY.'

Lavina's story reminded me of an experience I had with my dad just a few years ago. We were in a grocery store and three employees followed Dad around from the moment we entered. Eventually they stopped him, claimed they 'knew' he was attempting to steal a block of chocolate and asked to search his backpack. I was stunned, but Dad didn't even flinch. He simply unzipped his bag and flashed his New South Wales Police badge as an answer to their accusations.

There was some satisfaction in watching their faces drop as they realised they'd not only been caught out in their racial profiling, but had unknowingly done so to a police officer. My mum and I cried and yelled about it all the way home in the car, but Dad said nothing more than, 'It never changes. People like that never change.'

Being discriminated against your whole life because of your skin colour and being unable to escape it regardless of what you achieve or how hard you work is undeniably exhausting.

My dad has told me that time and time again when I've pressed him to be angrier, to do more; he's just sighed back at me, reminded me to be smart about picking my battles and told me he's tired of fighting.

I could see Lavina was tired too.

I guess the simple fact is, she shouldn't have had to be fighting anymore, she should have been able to just sit on that back porch, finish that mango and soak up the love of her family around her.

THAT'S WHAT LAVINA SAID HER GREATEST PASSION WAS, HER FAMILY. TO HER, THEY ARE EVERYTHING, AND IT'S OBVIOUS THE LOVE SHE HAS GIVEN HER GRANDCHILDREN AND GREAT-GRANDCHILDREN, IN PARTICULAR, IS WHAT WILL ENSURE THE FIGHT SHE HAS CARRIED FOR SO MUCH OF HER LIFE, WILL BE PASSED ON TO AND CARRIED FORWARD BY THEM.

I first heard about Lavina through her granddaughter Courtney. She'd reached out to me on our Tiddas 4 Tiddas Instagram account, wishing to publicly declare her admiration for her grandmother and to emphasise how much Lavina had inspired Courtney and her sisters, Amber and Lauren, with her strength.

THEY TOLD ME SHE IS THE LIGHT OF THEIR LIFE.

Shortly after writing this piece, I was informed that Lavina had recently lost her battle with cancer just an hour before her eighty-seventh birthday. It has been a true honour to be trusted by her amazing grandchildren and great-grandchildren to capture and publish a snippet of the incredible life she led.

LAVINA MIGHT'VE STRUGGLED TO SEE IT HERSELF, BUT IT IS WOMEN AND LEADERS LIKE HER THAT ARE THE BEST PART ABOUT BEING ABORIGINAL.

It is being able to learn from their struggle and be inspired to keep going no matter what, as they have in the face of such injustice and oppression. I'm sure her beautiful grandchildren and great grandchildren would agree with that.

WE, THE GENERATIONS THAT FOLLOW THEM, ARE ABLE TO DO MORE AND BE MORE BECAUSE OF THE PATHS OUR GRANDMOTHERS HAVE PAVED FOR US.

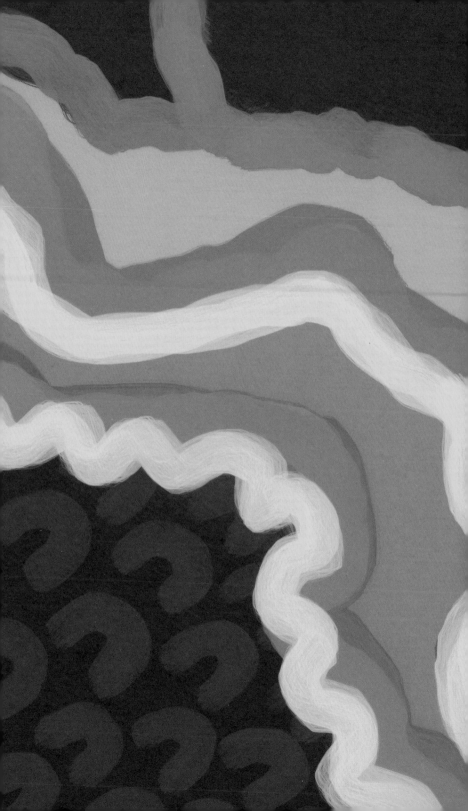

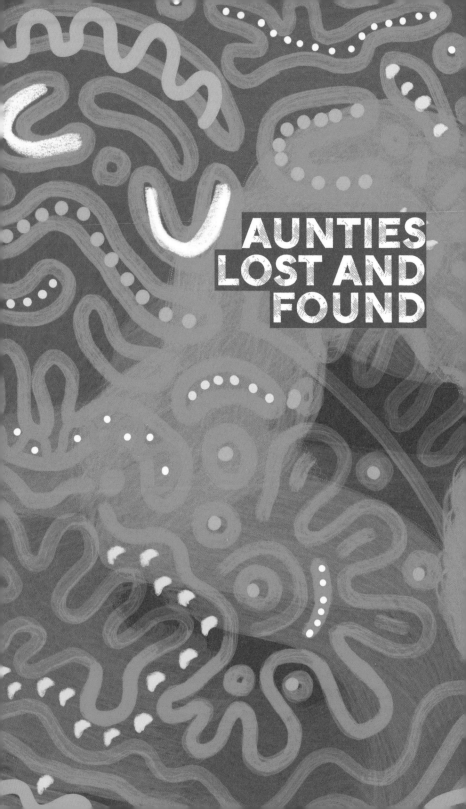

AUNTIES
LOST AND
FOUND

OLIVIA LUND
KAMILAROI, MURUWARI

SHANNAY HOLMES
DHARUG

I grew up envious of school mates and family friends who seemed so much more entrenched in their culture than I was. The ones who'd groan about going to Greek school on Saturday mornings, who could translate for their nonas struggling with English, and particularly my Maori friends, who'd move me to tears with every haka or story that seemed to flow from them with such ease.

I often felt inadequate, like I was failing my ancestors when stuttering through my perspective on Uncle Charlie Perkins' achievements with the Freedom Rides. Mind you, it was my year eight history teacher who'd asked me that, singling me out in class as the lone Aboriginal kid, which apparently appointed me as the representative and knowledge keeper of all things culture and history. It took me many years to realise how unfair it was and for my guilt in that and many other similar situations to subside.

What I know now is while traditional ceremonies and language were absent from my upbringing, my family takes much pride in stories and knowledge that we do have.

WHAT MY UNCLES, AUNTIES AND DAD WERE ABLE TO TEACH ME AND PASS DOWN IS MORE THAN MANY OTHERS HAVE; THEIR HISTORIES WERE RIPPED FROM THEIR BLOODLINES OR SWEPT UNDER THE RUG AS A RESULT OF THE STOLEN GENERATIONS.

The Stolen Generations not only bear the trauma of stolen identities; they also instilled a fear of outwardly identifying as Aboriginal, so as to avoid the mistreatment or theft of their babies.

This has left many Aboriginal and Torres Strait Islander people to grow up with little or no knowledge about their true history. So when I talk about our Aunties of the past, I too must talk about the lost Aunties. The ones whose grandchildren grew up not knowing them, who'd only heard whispers of their names, who were frustrated when questions were dismissed and left unanswered, or were startled by the presence of dark-skinned family in old pictures.

The journey back to these lost Aunties is unique for every individual who ventures through it. For the tiddas I've spoken to about this, the common element is an inherent sense of something missing, which is felt from a very young age.

Olivia Lund, now a twenty-three-year-old proud Kamilaroi and Muruwari woman, was a petite eight year old, swimming in her oversized school uniform, when a classmate said to her, 'We know you're Aboriginal.'

The strange accusation was blurted out in the midst of her peers making fun of her, and to Olivia the comment made no sense. As far as she was aware, she wasn't Aboriginal at all.

She asked her older sister on their walk home that day and she merely shrugged her shoulders and mumbled 'who knows' in response. For someone else, that might've been the end of it, but for Olivia, it firmly planted a seed of curiosity in her mind that would grow and grow in the years to come.

WHEN OLIVIA WAS FOURTEEN, SITTING IN THE SWEATY CARRIAGE OF A SYDNEY CITY RAIL TRAIN, A MIDDLE-AGED ABORIGINAL WOMAN CAUGHT HER EYE IN AMONG THE SEA OF SARDINE-PACKED COMMUTERS. AS THE NEXT STOP APPROACHED, THE WOMAN WHO'D BEEN WATCHING HER MOVED TOWARDS THE EXIT AND WAS PUSHED INTO OLIVIA BY THE HERD BEHIND HER. 'SORRY SIS!', SHE SAID SMILING APOLOGETICALLY AT OLIVIA, WHO SMILED BACK AND LET HER KNOW IT WAS ALL GOOD, NO WORRIES.

The woman paused, looking at her again and asked, 'Hey where's your mob from?' Olivia, startled, looked blankly back. The woman laughed and hopped off the train, and as she vanished into the crowded platform, Olivia's eight-year-old self appeared in the back of her mind.

By 2018, Olivia was in her second semester of university. After struggling to do a genogram on generations of her family, she couldn't handle being in the dark any longer and began investigating the truth about her family history. She started with immediate family. Her maternal grandmother had passed away before she could even raise the questions, but her grandfather had hinted that there had been times in their marriage when she'd mentioned Aboriginal heritage. Off the back of that Olivia went to her grandmother's sister, but she was completely shut down and was even deleted by her on Facebook.

If you're not in this situation, it's hard to understand Olivia's great aunt's reaction to a question about Aboriginality.

A friend of mine, a Dharug woman with a similar history to Olivia's, Shannay Holmes, helped me figure out such a reaction a little more by sharing with me the experiences her mum, grandparents and aunties have endured.

The Dharug mob, who come from what's known as Western Sydney today, have strong ties to the Hawkesbury River, which runs as a natural border between the Dharug people and neighbouring nations. It's here, along its banks, where Shannay's grandfather and his siblings were raised by his German father and black mother, on her traditional land. Shannay's pop, and his brothers and sister, were shades of brown that ranged from dark chocolate to caramel, but while there was some knowledge that their mum was Aboriginal, they were never allowed to talk about it and were sworn to secrecy.

Being raised in this way instilled a bitterness in Shannay's Pop. It's as if any time Aboriginality is mentioned, the voice of his late mother shushing him into silence rings loud in his ears, and he denies it altogether. This has caused some confrontation between Shannay and her pop. While she loves him dearly, she's had to push back on his reluctance, for the sake of her own identity and sense of belonging as well as that of her mother's.

As Shannay says, 'How can you pave your own future and know who you are with such a big part of you missing?

On the other hand, her pop's only sister could never ignore the gnawing hole in her identity and instead defied her mother's wishes by diving into their true history and becoming Shannay's family's champion of culture.

She was able to pass onto Shannay and her mum Jenny memories of her childhood that offered more of an explanation as to why the fear and anger around their blackness had manifested in such a way. She told them stories of her and her brothers being yelled at by their mum to run up and hide along the banks of the Hawkesbury River right by their house whenever a stranger would come by and their white dad wasn't home.

Through her own research, this aunty finally understood why they lived like this. It turns out her Aboriginal mother's father, Shannay's great-great-grandfather, was a victim of the Stolen Generations. He had been taken away from his family as a child, faced unimaginable trauma and when it came to his own kids, he'd passed on an intense and understandable fear of being taken too.

Thanks to Jenny's constant encouragement and yearning to learn more, Shannay has carried on her aunty's tradition of standing proud as a descendant of the Dharug people. Shannay has dedicated her career to working in and for community, and having grown up in Campbelltown in south-western Sydney, on Tharrawal country, she has been able to immerse herself even more in to her own blackness through the acceptance of local Elders.

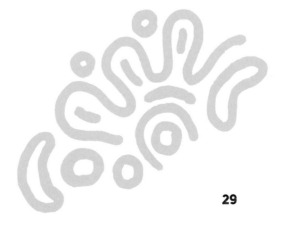

It has been a long and painful journey for Shannay and Jenny, especially when members of our own community question their Aboriginality at times. But Jenny is particularly thankful for her aunty and daughter's dedication. Jenny now works in mental health services with mostly Aboriginal clients and in coming into her true Aboriginal self, Shannay has seen her become so much more comfortable in her own skin. It's as if the fight to know who she is and what that means, which she's been having with herself for over forty years of life, is finally over.

ESTABLISHING A CONNECTION HAS COMPLETELY EMPOWERED JENNY. IT WAS MISSING FOR HER AND SHE FELT WHOLE WHEN SHE WAS FINALLY ABLE TO ACKNOWLEDGE IT.

It took me many years to realise the gaps in my knowledge were purposeful. That they were the lasting impacts from the generations before me, who were punished for speaking language, separated from their families and shamed or terrified into hiding traditions and stories deep within themselves. Before working this out, though, I often felt inadequate, like I was failing my ancestors when stuttering through my perspective on Uncle Charlie Perkins' achievements with the Freedom Rides. Mind you, it was my year eight history teacher who'd asked me that, singling me out in class as the lone Aboriginal kid, which apparently appointed me as the representative and knowledge keeper for a whole eighty thousand years of culture and history.

After the experience Olivia had with her great aunt, she felt like she'd hit a bit of a dead end with her mother's family, so started digging through her father's side too, not necessarily expecting to find Aboriginal ancestors there, but hungry to have answers to where she really came from either way. Eventually, she stumbled upon her great-grandfather, Hubert

Cameron, a soldier in World War I, and it was his enlistment documents that held the key to what she'd been searching for most of her life.

The main thing that stood out in the documents was a name: Hubert's mother, Nellie. She was listed as his next of kin, living at the Milgalarr Station on Hope Street, Warialda. When she talked to her family, Olivia's relatives didn't know Nellie existed. They were aware that her great grandfather's dad had remarried, but they didn't have any knowledge of who the previous woman was. The documents suggested Hubert Cameron was a child of the new wife, but this made no sense; it was physically impossible. So Olivia went back to documents and started digging some more and asking more questions. Eventually she confirmed Nellie was from Inverell, worked at the Milgalarr Station but was moved around to various places in her early life.

OLIVIA SAYS, 'AT TWENTY-THREE, I FOUND ME. I FOUND THE EXPLANATION FOR MY ACTIONS. FOR MY ENCOUNTERS. THIS MAY SOUND CLICHÉD, BUT I FELT WHOLE. FOR A LONG TIME, I HAVE FELT AS THOUGH I DIDN'T UNDERSTAND WHAT I WAS SEARCHING FOR, BUT NOW I KNOW. I KNOW WHY AT SIX YEARS OLD I WOULD RATHER RUN BAREFOOT AND FEEL THE EARTH BENEATH MY FEET. RUB THE SOIL AND SAND BETWEEN MY TOES AND CLOSE MY EYES. I KNOW WHAT I WAS SEARCHING FOR, AND THAT WAS ME.'

Despite this joy, Olivia also felt this overwhelming wave of guilt for not knowing sooner. She says she felt this immense sense of loss for Nellie, not like anything else she had ever known.

'It makes me cry when I think about how it makes me feel, but the best way I can put it into words is relief and pride.'

Olivia's biological response of needing to mourn Nellie is a testament to the unbreakable connection between Nellie and her descendent, Olivia.

THIS IS THE POWER OF OUR CULTURE. HOW IT CARRIES ON AND ON, THROUGH OUR BLOODLINES, NO MATTER WHETHER A NAME IS SPOKEN FOR GENERATIONS, OR A FULL STORY IS PASSED DOWN STRAIGHT AWAY AND UNFRAGMENTED.

While we might not all have to overcome the same obstacles in knowing our family heritage family that Olivia and Shannay have, what most humans have in common is an innate desire to confidently understand where they come from.

It is undeniable, Nellie has always been with Olivia. Calling her to come back, and now she will be known once more by Olivia's children and grandchildren. This is how we have always survived.

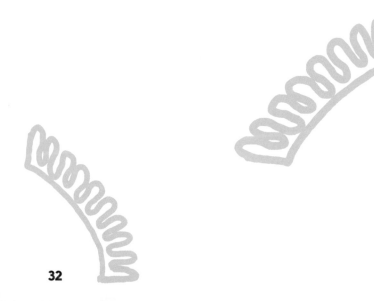

LIGHT-BLACK AND FULL OF SHIT – I MEAN, SALT | A POEM

The first time I saw a spoken-word poet
in 'real life', I mean not on YouTube, I mean
the first time I saw a spoken-word poet, I realised he was
full of shit.

This dude – hunched and heavy
with the weight of his drama
shuffled into my uni lecture and spluttered
stu t t t tered, and said
salt-salt-salt-salt
sixty times in sixty-salt seconds.
And they let him-salt
make-a-salt-book-salt.
A book for salt?
A real-salt-book, with his salt-name on it.
A real book for a dude, straight up full of salt.
I mean shit – full of shit.

Is the criteria for writing poetry – real poetry
must have experienced trauma?
Genuine question.
Trauma?
Rape?
Depression, oppression, discrimination?
Discrimination – great word.

Nation. Australia – what a nation.
Kamilaroi. Dunghutti. Nations.
My nations.
My people, ancestors, culture.

Surprise!
Light-coloured girl in front of you is actually
light-black.
Black where it counts, I say.
Black IN my body
IN my ability to make white-white men uncomfortable
am good at that
(must put on resume).

Light-black when white-white girls ask
why Dad is black-black.
TICK.
Light-black when I trip on my tongue
and bite back tears
when I can't remember the words
to explain to white-white classmates
why the word 'Abo' feels like, like
prodding hands in an open wound.
TICK.

Lighter-black when they tell me I'm a liar
not really black at all with that skin
even though – right then – I'd never felt blacker
'cause I know, in this nation
black – light or other
always comes after white-white.
TICK.

Just-black when white-white animals
growl 'Abo-tits' at me

and my shirt printed with my flag.
TICK.
Black-black when my poetry tutor tells me
my work sounds too intelligent
to be the voice of an Aborigine.
TICK.

BLACKEST when I still top his class
with a poem written in language.
TICK.
BLACKEST when I top all of my classes.
TICK.
BLACKEST when I get that job
when they call me CEO
when I sit across from that white-white politician man
in his white-white office in Canberra
and I tell him
I am black
I am proud
I am woman.
And I'm coming for his power.
TICK. TICK. TICK.

...

The first time I saw a spoken-word poet
in real life, I mean
I realised we're all full of shit.
I am full of salt – I mean shit.
I have a good life
I have not suffered.
But I guess a salt-white-white dude in my lecture
hunched with the weight of his drama
pisses me off
because he finds it easy

to locate his sadness in a lived event.
I am jealous because
a psychiatrist can pinpoint that moment
work with him through it
work him towards healing.

What do you prescribe for
a depression rooted in family history?
A sadness born before my conception.
A darkness written onto my future genes
when my great-grandmother
miscarried in her husband's arms
when an ambulance refused to come
onto the mission where they lived.
It was practically tattooed on my grandmother
as she had her black-black skin spat on
by classmates
every single day of high school.
When she and my grandfather lost their first son
because of a polio vaccine he was denied.
Cemented in every fibre of my father's hurt
that's something I simply cannot speak about.

How do I unwrite it?
How can I fix me?
Us?

I guess I'll just have to learn to survive
as they did
as something full of salt
I mean shit.

LET'S TALK ABOUT
JANUARY 26

January 26. Australia Day. Invasion Day. Survival Day.

No matter what you call it, we can all agree there's no other date on the calendar that divides the country with the same intensity as this one.

This debate over what day of the year is most appropriate to celebrate Australia, or whether Australia Day is worth celebrating at all, is one of the most emotionally distressing and socially ostracising topics that I and most of my Indigenous brothers and sisters are forced to face every single year.

So, the question for us, as both Indigenous and non-Indigenous people of this country, is how do we best equip ourselves for it? What can we do to support each other and make getting through the day and the conversations leading up to it a little easier and more productive for all?

1. UNDERSTAND THE HISTORY

- January 26 marks the anniversary of the First Fleet sailing into Port Jackson in 1788 and raising the Union Jack for the first time, falsely claiming stolen Aboriginal land for the King of England. This kickstarted the following two centuries of unimpeded genocide, slavery, theft and murder of Aboriginal and Torres Strait Islander people.

- The first-ever national day was celebrated on 30 July 1915, not in recognition of the establishment of the colonies, but instead to raise money for the World War I effort. 'Australia Day' itself was only formalised as a national holiday in 1994, and prior to this all states and territories celebrated on different dates. In short, changing what it means and when it's held is nothing new or difficult.

- Aboriginal people have been advocating against January 26 since before it was declared a national day of celebration, with Jack Patten, William Ferguson and William Cooper having called for it to be considered a Day of Mourning in 1938.

- Many migrant communities and other non-white groups also feel uncomfortable about celebrating the day, as it is frequently accompanied by demonstrations of xenophobia from conservative folk who believe that to be Australian you must be 'white'.

2. PUT RESPECT FIRST

Dear non-Indigenous friends, YES, it is fantastic that you want to learn more and build a stronger perspective of this debate. We encourage you to take the time to read and listen to Indigenous voices. But NO, not every Aboriginal or Torres Strait Islander person is going to feel comfortable as a spokesperson for the day. Respect their decision to talk about it – or not.

3. TIDDAS AND BALAS, YOUR NUMBER ONE PRIORITY AT THIS TIME OF THE YEAR IS TO LOOK AFTER YOURSELF!

- Say NO when you don't feel up to engaging with the discussion.
- Stay away from the comments sections on social media posts related to the day.
- Surround yourself with people you can trust.
- Attend black events.
- Cry if you have to.
- And especially, if you need it, ask for help.

As far as my opinions regarding the day go, I'll say I love Australia, even with all the scars and wounds that come with it, but I cannot separate January 26 from its direct linkage to my people's suffering for over two centuries. I will never be able to celebrate this continent as it exists today on that date.

It is important to stress, though, I will still feel unable to celebrate Australia on any day, if the date change isn't accompanied by a change in attitudes and actions. To me, a large part of the problem is the national identity crisis we have. Being a country built on a lie in 'terra nullius' (land belonging to nobody) and on such violence, Australia's troubled foundations cloud any understanding of what it means to be Australian.

The most important next step is not just changing the date, but changing how we perceive ourselves and how we relate to one another, through our values and respect for differences.

— | PART II | —

TIDDAS PRESENT

*Without my sisters beside me, I am
not whole, nor are any of my individual
achievements possible. This chapter celebrates
those staunch females who have helped build me
(and my platform of Tiddas 4 Tiddas) to where
I am today. These tiddas have done so through their
unashamed vulnerability, rawness and resilience. They
have ignited the fire within me, and so many others, to
work harder every day and to reach further. They remind
us of what's important, putting our circumstances into
perspective, and consistently help us all believe we
are stronger and more capable than we know.*

DEADLY TIDDA
noun

A strong Indigenous woman. Go-getter,
sophisticated, smart mouth. Holds it down,
spiritual soul. Confident, always ready to help
another tidda win. Has a big heart like no other.
And a lil' bit of hood 'bout her!
(via @ginnysgirlgang Instagram)

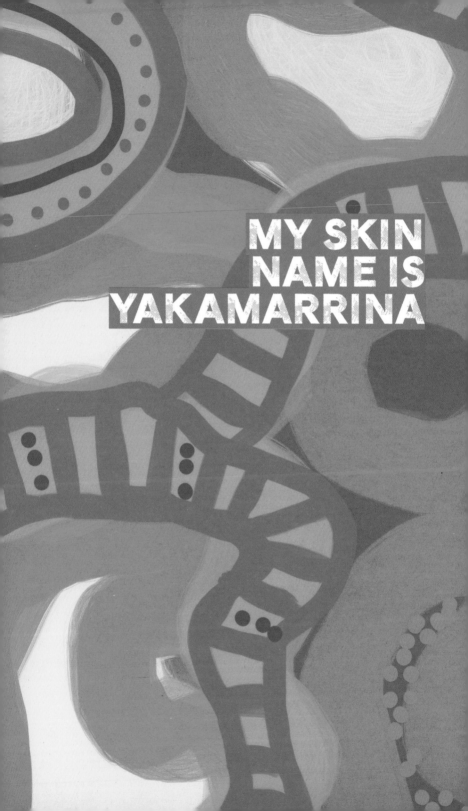

MY SKIN
NAME IS
YAKAMARRINA

JOLA CUMMING
BUTCHELLA, GARAWA SALT WATER

A skin name is a cultural name that is gifted to some Aboriginal people by the Elders of their mob and it's traditionally helped distinguish the roles of individuals in their family. Be they knowledge keepers or medicine men or women, their skin name helps everyone understand their place.

Twenty-four-year-old Jola Cumming is a proud Butchulla and Garawa Salt Water Murri woman. Her mobs come from Hervey Bay and the Gulf of Carpentaria, and when she tells me her skin name, her voice shifts. It's as if her tongue is relieved by how natural it feels, as the soft syllables trickle off it. Her face lights up too. I can feel the weight it carries for her, and wonder what the other pockets of strangers in the dimly lit cafe we've met in would think if they knew how hard she'd fought to be able to carry on this eighty-thousand-year-old tradition, with such a name.

You see, Jola's always known she is Aboriginal, but it's only been in recent years that she's come to better understand what it means. As a child, Jola and her older brother Isaiah were forcibly removed from their family, which resulted in them spending most of their childhood growing up in the small New South Wales country town of Yass, on Ngunnawal land, thousands of kilometres south of their country.

I FIRST HEARD ABOUT JOLA THROUGH ISAIAH. HE AND I WERE SPEAKING AT THE SAME EVENT, TELLING OUR RESPECTIVE STORIES. WE WERE YARNING ABOUT WHAT LIGHTS THE FIRES THAT BURN IN OUR BELLIES, TO MAKE CHANGE FOR OUR PEOPLE, AND I SWEAR AS HE SPOKE, NOBODY IN THE ROOM MADE A SOUND.

Yes, Isaiah is an exceptional orator, but what stops his audiences in their tracks is the truth revealed in what he's saying. The trauma and the hurdles these two young blackfullas have been through, detached from family, from their identity and their sense of belonging, is horrifying – even more so when you consider they are two out of thousands of Aboriginal and Torres Strait Islander children in care in 2019 – and accentuates the absolute resilience and power they hold within them.

When I sat down with Jola, I opened with the same question I always do, 'Who's your mob and where are you from?' After we'd warmed up for a few minutes, I regretted that. She told me she actually used to hate being asked that exact question, given it was at age twenty-three that she was reunited with her grandmothers, aunties, uncles and mum for the first time.

Identity, is a tricky path to navigate for all of us, but imagine growing up, trying to figure out who you are and what that means, when you don't have a parent or blood relative to turn to. Nobody to answer the questions. And at times, as Jola revealed, she had carers that took in her and Isaiah who were meant to protect and look after them, but instead they told them that their culture and heritage was something to be ashamed of. That their skin wasn't brown, but dirty.

In year ten, Jola was accepted as a boarding student at an affluent school in Sydney, and although she and her brother had been surviving the day to day with each other to lean on, this is where that surviving turned to thriving.

She won't deny there were tough times throughout her final years of school, particularly when, in the middle of the school term, the two siblings were notified unexpectedly that they were no longer welcome at their foster carers' residence and were, in turn, left homeless.

Despite this and the plenty of other times when she felt close to giving up on graduating, Jola held on. Jola attributes her ability to do so to a female role model at school, an Indigenous support officer named Kim, who pushed her to get there. At the time, being so young, Jola acknowledges she probably gave Kim a bit of cheek and didn't even realise how important the belief Kim had in her was. But in hindsight Jola holds so much appreciation for the relationship she and Kim had and how it shaped her future:

'Now, I'm so grateful that she saw that graduating would be life changing for me … I guess all you need is that one person to believe in you to make it through, and she was that person. She was like no, you're staying, you're staying. I wouldn't have gone to university if she didn't get me to graduation.'

Jola has since become the first in her family to graduate from university. Not only with a Bachelor Degree in Health Science, but a Masters of Education too, which will see her undertake a career dedicated to uplifting the next generation through education. Although she acknowledges that structured education and university isn't for everyone, Jola asserts that there's nothing more powerful than holding knowledge.

'GROWING UP, HAVING A LOT OF THINGS TAKEN AWAY FROM ME – FAMILY, CULTURAL IDENTITY – ONE THING THAT I'VE MADE SURE NO-ONE CAN TAKE AWAY FROM ME IS MY KNOWLEDGE ... KNOWLEDGE IS POWER. I THINK THE MOST DANGEROUS THING IN THE WORLD IS TO BE A KNOWLEDGEABLE BLACK WOMAN. YOU CAN'T GET BETTER THAN THAT.'

The defining factor in her pursuit of teaching is that it's enabled her to empower young Indigenous women. For many of us living in Australia, we spend the majority of our first eighteen years in a classroom, and what happens within the walls of the classroom or school environment has significant influence on our understanding and acceptance of ourselves.

The power of having a teacher in the front of a classroom who looks like you or comes from your culture, and can empathise with your circumstances, should not be underestimated. So by being there and being able to speak with tenderness and consideration to kids with diverse backgrounds, particularly around discussions concerning family structures and identity or belonging, Jola will hold the power to change lives.

In the face of adversity, to me, the true leaders and the ones I strive to be like are those who emerge without bitterness and have an insatiable desire to give back, and ensure nobody goes through what they have. That's what Jola represents to me.

She told me how the fact that only two other Aboriginal girls made it to graduation at her high school really frustrated her. The numbers weren't good enough in her mind, and she will hold higher expectations for her students, as she empowers them with a sense of self pride, of confidence and life skills, on top of educational knowledge.

Jola strives to support young people in a holistic, well-rounded way because she knows that if expectations are held higher than the bare minimum, if our young people are believed in and given the right support and opportunities, they do not simply pass school, and they don't sit with the average. No, what they really do is, 'They kill it.'

'YOU CAN DO IT ALL ON YOUR OWN, SISTER!'

JACINTA MARSHALL

ARRENTE, WULUWURRA, ALYAWARRA, KALKADOON

Jacinta is a psychologist, a mother, aunty and advocate who is utterly dedicated to making positive change for her people. Among the staunch calls for an end to casual, systemic and structural racism as well as concerns with lateral violence – or 'tall poppy syndrome' that we see within our own Indigenous community – Jacinta also spoke to me about one of the next goals in her already accomplished life, which is to focus on healing herself, so as not to pass pain on to her children.

This struck me. Healing is a concept we discuss quite a lot in our community, mostly I think, because it's what we yearn for. It's what I'd argue is the most vital step in making progress in any area of our way of being. Complex issues that impact us all emerge from an open wound.

If you've ever come across a bully in school or the workplace, you would've heard people talk about them as most likely having been bullied themselves and that causes them to treat other people poorly, as a projection or deflection of their own perceptions of inadequacy. Now, I'm not an expert of the mind like Jacinta is, but through my relationships and interactions with others this perception of the 'bully' rings true. Negative actions, whether it be to oneself or others, are made by an individual when they're hurting.

So how do we heal? How do we become aware of the trauma that lives in us, how it impacts the way we move in the world, and soothe it in order to emerge as our fiercest and best selves?

For starters, I think we need to release any shame we hold in feeling such pain or sadness. As women in particular, no matter our colour or background, we're told that our emotions and our hurt are our weakness. It makes us soft, not strong. For me personally, in becoming aware of hurt that existed within myself, I felt as though I had no right to feel the way I did. I felt that my 'suffering' was nothing in comparison to others, nor the suffering of my aunties and grandmothers who came before me.

Intergenerational trauma speaks of the genetic effect that trauma has on a person's DNA. It explains that when those generations before us experienced horror, it was written on the cells that would be passed on to their future children, grandchildren and so on. I was trying to understand that better when I wrote 'Light-black and Full of Shit – I Mean, Salt.' I felt guilty about my mental health and the wound that remained open inside of me. But there is no shame in that, there's only shame in giving up and believing you can do nothing to heal or change it.

FOLLOWING ACCEPTANCE OF THE HURT, COMES ACTION. JACINTA TALKS ABOUT LEANING ON HER FAMILY TO FILL HER HEART AND REMIND HER THAT THINGS WILL ALWAYS GET BETTER. PUTTING THE STRENGTH OF IDENTITY, OUR ANCESTORS AND CONNECTION TO COUNTRY AT THE CENTRE OF YOUR FOCUS, AND OWNING YOUR POWER, ARE VITAL STEPS IN THE CONTINUAL JOURNEY OF HEALING.'

This incredible tidda has offered me such deep inspiration in her dedication to fight, for us as a people, her family and herself. It is her greatest purpose in life, to selflessly dedicate all her energy to securing a future of positive prosperity for everyone.

On top of that I feel the genuine care she holds for every single one of us blakfullas and how personally pleasing she finds it when one of us succeeds. The generosity she demonstrates in passing on so much of what she's learnt is a powerful reminder to all of us: as we move along in our own journeys, gaining knowledge through our experiences, one we reach the other side we shouldn't act as gatekeepers who keep those lessons to ourselves; we should share them with those who follow us. When we break through the door before us, we should look back and hold it open for the one behind us, for the sisters coming after us. This will not detract from our struggles, instead it will strengthen our collective progress.

In the words she sent me, Jacinta finished her story with advice she'd like to give to other women and girls. Jacinta is so nurturing, the beauty and power of her conviction is best delivered in her own words, so here they are for you:

RISE UP MY SISTERS, RISE UP.

Empower each other and build up each other's self-worth. Our lack of self-worth and self-esteem helps others to pit us against each other, instead of supporting each other. We need to see each other as allies and not enemies.

- *Easier said than done, but women don't realise how strong they really are. We are the backbones of community, and our health and wellbeing is the health and wellbeing of our families and our communities.*

- *A lot of the time, I think our inability to support each other comes from our own insecurities. When we are insecure about ourselves we lash out against each other, rather than supporting one another and building each other up. It's a hard pill to swallow and something I work on each day, but I think it is something else to consider when we're thinking about how we can support each other.*

TO ALL SISTERS – OWN YOUR POWER.

- *Surround yourself with good people, people who want the best for you. Know your worth and believe that we see you! We see you trying every day and we are rooting for you to succeed. You hold the key to the future you want for yourself, your children and your future generations. Don't be afraid to own up to your mistakes, or to lean on others for support because we all make mistakes and need help in our lives.*

- *You can do it all on your own, sister!*

- *Finally, put the hard work in now to save you from having to work twice as hard down the track.*

'I KNOW HOW IMPORTANT IT IS TO BE PROUD OF YOUR IDENTITY'

KIYA WATT
MENANG, GNUDJU, NOONGAR

You see a young woman in the street, your local shops, a doctor's surgery, anywhere. She couldn't be more than seventeen and she's obviously pregnant. She's all on her own too.

What comes to your mind in that moment? Do you think she's got much of a future ahead of her? How do you feel when I tell you she's actually expecting twins and their father isn't around anymore?

This is Kiya Watt's story, a Menang, Gnudju, Noongar woman and artist. The Noongar nation is the southern region of Western Australia and is made up of fourteen different language and tribe groups. Menang and Gnudju are two of them.

I was introduced to Kiya's name and face when a new Aboriginal character was announced on the iconic ABC children's show *Play School*. Kiya had designed the beautiful dress of a little dolly, who shares her name, and would be introduced to the show to help the next generation of Australian children connect with our culture.

IT WAS A LANDMARK EVENT IN TERMS OF OUR REPRESENTATION ON AUSTRALIAN TV. HAVING ABORIGINAL AND TORRES STRAIT ISLANDER CULTURE INTRODUCED TO AUSTRALIAN CHILDREN EARLY IN LIFE IS OUR BEST BET IN ENSURING WE'RE EMBEDDED IN THE EVERYDAY, THAT WE'RE FAMILIAR. KNOWING NOW THAT THIS MOMENT WAS DRIVEN BY A MUM OF THREE, WHO WAS TOLD SHE'D NEVER AMOUNT TO MUCH, IS THE INSPIRATIONAL CHERRY ON TOP.

Kiya told me the following story just flowed out of her on a long bus ride to Perth, on her way to an art exhibition. It is raw and powerful, and it is her truth.

Thank you Kiya.

'To my father, thank you for holding your head high in a society that was trying to keep you down. Your pride in who you are has been carried on to your children. You are our greatest gift. And to my mum for standing by me throughout all stages in my life and helping me raise proud children. I would not be the person I am today without you.

'I grew up in Denmark, a really small town located in south Western Australia, where there were only two Aboriginal families other than ours, and school was dominated by non-Indigenous people.

'I remember whenever there was any Aboriginal history taught in school or videos played (which were very limited) I would always hear kids laughing and I would feel so embarrassed. There was never any representation of successful Indigenous people. They only showed Aboriginal people battling addiction or in the bush.

'I remember one time at a school camp, there was this group of kids who kept singing, *I like boongs, boongs like me. Fat ones, skinny ones, I like boongs.* At the time, I didn't know what it really meant, but I just remember feeling from an early age that being Aboriginal was something to be embarrassed about. Because of the shame, I would straighten my hair and ask that my dad didn't come to my school events because I just wanted to fit in.

'When high school came, I was angry and just felt like I was never enough. I tried really hard to be "cool" and started drinking, doing drugs and skipping school a lot. I started really taking my anger out on my father and blaming him for a lot of my issues.

'At that age I couldn't pinpoint the effects of having an identity crisis, but now can look back and realise how badly I was acting out because of these issues.

'It ended up being too much for my father to handle, and rightfully so, I was basically out of control so I moved to Albany to live with my mother.

'At this stage I was around fifteen and drinking every weekend. At least in Albany there were Aboriginal people like me. A lot of them would come up to me at parties or at high school and say your nan or your pop is my family, and I just remember feeling torn … like I belonged but I was filled with a different kind of shame. I felt shame that I never knew these people who were related to me, as my father was taken from his mother due to the white assimilation policy.

'I felt like I couldn't really fit in anywhere. I just became more insecure, which led to me needing attention and eventually, a boyfriend. Around sixteen, I fell into an unhealthy and abusive relationship. Throughout it, I remember always blaming myself and trying so hard to make this person love me. I became careless and at seventeen, I fell pregnant.

'Do you know how over represented Indigenous teen pregnancies are in Australia? One in four teen mums in Australia is Indigenous, and I truly believe this is because of the shame and trauma that affects us mob still today.

'No matter how broken and low my self-esteem was, I was actually happy about being pregnant. My boyfriend was also happy at the time, and I felt like I had done the right thing by keeping him happy, and thought he'd love me even more now that I was having his child. To my surprise, at eight weeks pregnant I got an ultrasound and was told I was having twins.

'At first, I really took pride in my pregnancy. But it wasn't long after I started showing, when I would have people come up to me and tell me 'I was stupid', 'I had ruined my life' or 'my life was over'. Even at the hospital, a few of the midwives and staff would look at me and shake their heads. It played a huge part in making me feel like I was a failure.

'After I had my twins sons, their father cheated on me, fell into drugs and left. Then, I was eighteen and isolated, with two babies.

'IT TOOK ME YEARS TO FINALLY FEEL LIKE MYSELF AGAIN AND WHEN [MY KIDS] WERE FOUR, I STARTED STUDYING. THAT WAS WHEN I TRULY STARTED TO BECOME MORE AWARE OF HOW IMPORTANT EDUCATION WAS. I STUDIED COMMUNITY SERVICES AND ENDED UP GETTING A DIPLOMA.

'I also now a have a little girl and I'm raising my children as a single mother. But for the first time in my life I am completely confident and okay with being single and raising my children. I am not insecure and I know I don't need anyone to feel worthy or successful.

**'EVERYTHING I WENT THROUGH MADE
ME GROW AND I AM HAPPY I HAVE THIS
EXPERIENCE IN LIFE NOW, AS I KNOW HOW
IMPORTANT IT IS TO BE PROUD OF YOUR
IDENTITY.**

'I have reconnected with my biological family and learnt my [D]reaming stories and that's what I do now.

'I am an Aboriginal artist and I paint my stories and do workshops with children to help them feel proud. I hope by sharing my story I can raise awareness around the impacts of having no cultural identity or pride in who you are.'

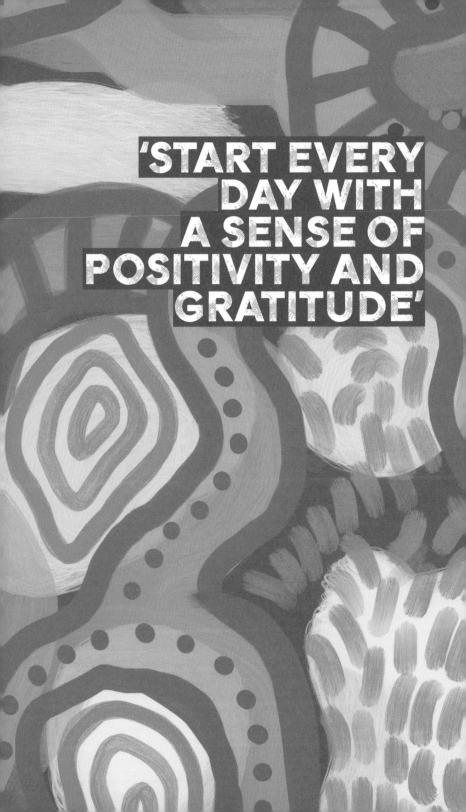

'START EVERY DAY WITH A SENSE OF POSITIVITY AND GRATITUDE'

ADINA AND LIBBY BROWN
BIRIPI, GUMBAYNGGIRR, YUIN

Adina Brown, a twenty-year-old Biripi, Gumbaynggirr and
Yuin woman, was a defining inspiration behind my
creation of Tiddas 4 Tiddas. She came into my life in 2018
as a stand-out player in the under eighteen's Indigenous
Australian Representative Oztag team in that year's World
Cup Tournament.

My sister Keely and I coached and managed the team
throughout the competition, and although Adina is
undeniably an impressive athlete, that wasn't what set
her apart from the rest of the players for me. It was her
natural leadership on and off the field, her ability to remain
positive even in the toughest moments and, most of all, her
unrelenting kindness and generosity in the way she treated
every person she interacted with.

As most females will know or have experienced, in a group
setting teenage girls can be quite cliquey and jealous, which
can lead to division and tension, with one or more of the girls

feeling left out or alone. That was something I was worried about when I began working with this team; if any social problems were going to arise, there's no way the team would be successful, not just in winning games but in having a great experience overall. One of the things I hoped they'd get out of it the most was connecting with other like-minded blackfullas going through the same stuff as they were, as I'd been given those opportunities at the same age and valued them above almost everything else.

Thankfully, though, almost as if she'd anticipated it herself, when the girls all met each other for the first time, Adina took the initiative to build personal connections with all sixteen of them.

BEFORE WE'D EVEN PICKED UP A FOOTBALL, SHE WAS LAYING THE FOUNDATIONS FOR A STRONG, UNITED TEAM, WHERE EVERYONE'S VOICE AND ROLE MATTERED.

Coming back home after the competition, the seed that had been planted within me earlier that year – to start something that celebrated Aboriginal and Torres Strait Islander women – grew and grew to a point where I could no longer simply just think about it.

IN THE SHORT TIME I'D KNOWN ADINA, I WAS CONVINCED SHE WAS PRETTY SPECIAL AND SHE'D LEFT ME FEELING EXCITED FOR HER PERSONAL, AND OUR COLLECTIVE, FUTURE.

Being surrounded by Adina and the other inspiring young women in our team proved to me that what I had been thinking was correct. In light of the conversations we had with them, it was clear that so many amazing stories of our mob were being missed, and that so many young females were hungry to hear them, wanting to learn more about themselves and their place in the world.

So, within a week, Tiddas 4 Tiddas went live.

I believe Adina has so much lying ahead of her that when I went travelling in the middle of 2019 and wanted a break from constant social media access and phone contact, I trusted her to take over our Tiddas 4 Tiddas Instagram and Facebook accounts. I told her to use the page to post about whatever mattered to her and to share stories or thoughts and ideas she felt other Aboriginal women and girls would benefit from thinking about.

From her first post, I knew I'd put my faith in the right person and even learnt a new tool I now use to realign myself when the world gets a bit loud and chaotic:

> 'Starting every day with a sense of positivity and gratitude can change your mood and mindset completely. Reminding yourself that what makes you happy and grateful can influence your perspective dramatically. Everyday jotting down or even thinking about three things we are grateful for and three things we are looking forward to can contribute to a positive mindset. Tag us in your daily mindfulness and let us know how doing this has made you feel!'

What are the ingredients to making such a thoughtful young role model? How is it that someone can form such mature and considered perspectives on everyday action so early on? The answer unsurprisingly came to me through Adina's mum Libby.

ADINA TOLD ME HER MUM AND DAD ARE HER BIGGEST ROLE MODELS AND THEY'D RAISED HER AND HER THREE BROTHERS WITH A DEEP KNOWLEDGE OF WHAT IT MEANS TO BE ABORIGINAL, A KNOWLEDGE THAT CAME TO THEM THROUGH THEIR FAMILY HISTORIES.

Her parents continuously emphasised how the sacrifice and hardship their ancestors faced had led to the opportunities their family have been afforded today. Libby runs a business called Aboriginal Counselling, which uses culturally specific support tools to help Aboriginal and Torres Strait Islander clients with their social and emotional wellbeing. Her passion for improving Aboriginal health outcomes and the heart with which she helps people through tough times, in particular, comes from her own mother, who dedicated her life to caring for Koori kids in foster care.

During thirty-four years as a foster carer, Libby's mum looked after more than one hundred and fifty children. She believed in keeping Aboriginal kids in their families and communities and was determined to see them keep their birth names; it was important to be honest with them about their birth families and their past so they could always find their way back home. To her, neither she nor anyone else could ever own children, they were just on loan to her, and she often said,

'OUR JOB AS ADULTS IS TO CARE FOR THEM AND LOVE THEM.'

For a period of time, Libby and her mother were homeless, but through unwavering determination and hard work, she was evenually able to buy a house, and continued to give back to her community with everything she had, giving space to those young ones who needed it. Libby was raised watching matriarchal leadership and black resilience in motion; it revealed her own power to her, helping her to continue her mother's spirit and instilling the same positive and generous values in her that we see Adina express today.

I have no doubt that both Adina and Libby will be spending the rest of their lives continuing to give all of themselves to what matters to them most: their culture and the prosperity of our people.

THEY BOTH TALK ABOUT HOW THEY COULDN'T IMAGINE BEING ANYTHING OTHER THAN ABORIGINAL AND HOW THEIR ABORIGINALITY ACTS AS A GUIDING STAR FOR EACH DECISION THEY MAKE.

I hope their attitude continues to inspire blackfullas everywhere to feel the same way and to know the great beauty and excellence that comes with being part of the oldest continuous surviving culture in history.

For the past few years, I've proudly watched from the sidelines as Adina has flourished at university and is coming into her own as an emerging leader, learning to raise her voice more and more about the issues and subjects she cares about most. So it's fitting that her voice has its own spotlight in this story of hers – and of the two generations of strong females before her.

The following is a letter she wrote to her future self:

Dear future me,

Never give up, keep pushing through. Your education is key, use your knowledge and past experience as a tool to help others. Lead and empower the people around you. Keep pushing – the sun will always rise and the world will go on, keep smiling because you are happy, healthy and loved.

MOTIVATE AND BE MOTIVATED. STRIVE TO BE A BETTER PERSON DAY BY DAY, WHETHER IT'S BIG OR SMALL. BE SELFLESS AND KIND, LOOK FOR INSPIRATION AND ALWAYS REMEMBER IT'S OKAY TO TAKE SOME TIME FOR YOURSELF TO REFOCUS.

Enjoy your time with family and friends. Any drama around you is so worthless considering how quickly time goes on, the negatives are forgotten but your loved ones should not be.

Spread love & kindness, be passionate and confident. Use your past experience whether its pain, happiness or confusion as a lesson to help others and yourself with life's challenges.

Just remember everything will be okay, so just persevere and be positive with everything.

Love past Adina

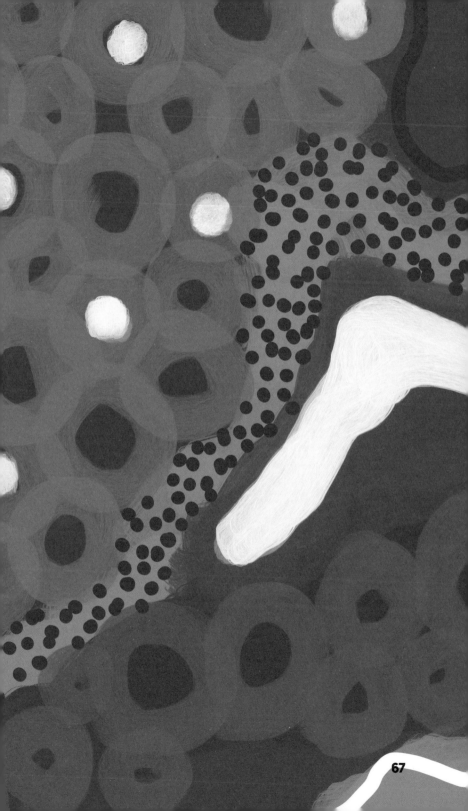

'LEARN WHO YOU ARE, WHAT YOUR STRENGTH AND PURPOSE IS, AND YOU WILL SEE YOU ARE INVINCIBLE.'

CHLOE QUAYLE
MALYANGAPA

Chloe Quayle is a twenty-four-year-old Malyangapa woman from the Barkindji nation, she's a mother, a jewellery maker and a business woman. At the core of the success she has gained is her ability to defy the odds, to overcome the enormous obstacles she has faced in her past and to prove the statistics and expectations held against her to be completely wrong.

Chloe developed an addiction to the drug known as 'ice' when she was fifteen years old. It came about shortly after the birth of her first child, when she was spending time with a crowd of people who had a bad influence on her. At this point in her life she was convinced she was worthless and that drugs and alcohol were her only escape.

> *'I'd stay up for five days and when I'd come down, I'd feel really suicidal. I was just torn apart thinking about the person I was.'*

The drug made her violent, getting her into trouble with the law early on. She was in and out of juvenile detention and had her children taken from her. Her health deteriorated significantly, and, as she reflects now, the addiction had a heavy toll on her family relationships too. Lying to her mum about her addiction is something about which she still feels particular guilt and regret.

At twenty-one, while pregnant with her youngest son, she ended up being locked up for assaulting a police officer. That served as the turning point on the path she was going down; things would otherwise have likely been very different, ending with the loss of her life.

I FIRST CAME ACROSS CHLOE'S STORY THROUGH A FACEBOOK POST SHE'D WRITTEN THAT WAS GOING VIRAL.

In the post, she detailed the trauma she faced as a pregnant incarcerated woman, and the harshness of the discrimination and disregard for her human rights struck me intensely. The honesty in her words, the reality of prison life and the pride and strength she showed in reclaiming her identity were truly moving and obviously inspiring to many across social media.

'Having my little fulla in custody was the hardest thing I've ever had to go through and my biggest wake-up call ... I remember applying for Jacaranda, the mums and bubs prison, and getting knocked back because I only had three months to go and I didn't have much longer to serve.

I was so used to having my babies with me and taking them home with me, I felt like my heart was ripped out of me when I had to leave my son 3 days later in the hospital and got taken back to the jail. I remember wanting to breast feed him at the visits but the prison officer said to me "Put it away, there's no need for that" with disgust written all over his face. I remember coming back to the compound trying to hold it in but as soon as I saw the sisters I broke down in tears. They all cuddled me while I cried and told me I'll get through this and they cried with me.

THAT SUPPORT CARRIED ME THROUGH MY SENTENCE.

A week after giving birth to my son they put me on a job of concreting for the prison, getting paid $23 a week. I was told if I quit they'd take me off phone calls, buy ups and visits... My body couldn't take the hard labour and I started losing massive amounts of blood and got really sick. I literally had to be bleeding to death for them to let my body and heart heal after giving birth to my baby. There's no counsellors in prison either.

The system won't change anytime soon, the system is against my people! If they can't colonise us, they will incarcerate us! New age slavery. I will not be known by 528213 ever again, my name is Chloe Quayle, even with the odds against me like every black mother in the system, I love my jarjums! I will never ever put them or myself through that again and I won't give the system the satisfaction of seeing me fail.'

For the broader Australian community, jail is a concept almost too hard to comprehend, it is so removed from their reality. Many people go through life without having any connection to anyone who has been inside, but, for us blackfullas, it is something we know far too well. Aboriginal and Torres Strait Islander people are severely over-represented in the incarceration system; we are criminalised young, institutionalised and, once released, due to the stigma we face and the inadequate support we receive, many of us struggle to ever fully settle back into society.

These stats and the stories that come with them mean the expectations for anyone who ends up in goal are extremely low, and to overcome the obstacles and beat the odds is a phenomenal thing to achieve.

At twenty-one and a half, after the final fourteen-month sentence she would serve, Chloe got clean and promised never to put herself or her young family through the horror of drugs and gaol again. When she got out, she was so comforted by the response from her family:

> 'It was nice to hear my mum because for so long I disappointed her, so it was so comforting to hear that my family was happy I was home.'

With the addiction behind her, Chloe said she felt so liberated and empowered, having reclaimed control over her life. Her bravery and strength cannot be understated. It's very easy to call drug users 'losers' and refuse to offer empathy, thinking they've done it to themselves, but human beings are all inherently flawed. We don't know every individual's situation; we're allowed to make mistakes and learn from them, to be better and do better for the ones we love.

Since her recovery, Chloe has lived in Parramatta with her children Alinta, Amaroo and Aziah. In all, she remains close with her family, having gone into partnership with her mum in an Aboriginal jewellery–making business. When I reached out to Chloe to see if she wanted to share this story with me, she jumped at the opportunity. She wants everyone to know her story, to know that anyone can make it through the darkest of times, just as she did.

HER BABIES WERE HER STRENGTH AND THE DRIVING FORCE FOR HER TO MAKE A CHANGE.

No matter the obstacle you face, whether it be addiction, mental health issues or even low expectations or low self-esteem, you can overcome it. Learn who you are, what your strength and purpose is, and you will see you are invincible.

That's what Chloe's story tells me, and by sharing it with the world so bravely and with so much rawness, she's been able to rewrite her narrative, and help rewrite our collective narrative as a people, as one of triumph rather than defeat.

'I'm glad I put my story out there online, because there's always that sad story, especially in Aboriginal communities, where drugs have come in and ripped families and communities apart. The media portrays us as drunks and addicts and you don't really hear the good stories. It's really nice because I see girls tag their friends and say, "we can do it", and you can. There is a life after drugs.'

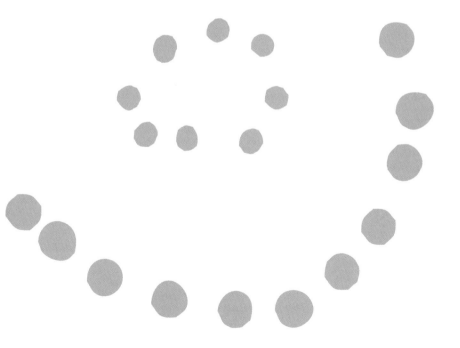

'BE PROUD OF YOUR CULTURE AND THE ANCESTORS THAT WALK AND GUIDE YOU THROUGH THIS JOURNEY OF LIFE'

TAMIKA SADLER
SOUTH SEA ISLANDER

Mother, business owner, student, writer, climate activist,
Aboriginal, Torres Strait and South Sea Islander woman.

For a woman in her early twenties, Tamika Sadler has more
titles attached to her name than many are ever likely to
have. She's also worked harder than most, overcoming great
obstacles to achieve those titles. Some time ago, Tamika and
I worked for the same company, and I remember the first time
I met her so clearly. She seemed to glow with such warmth
and happiness, I knew instantly that she must have a kind
heart. I could tell that she considered every word she said for
the impact it might have.

As the eldest of five children, Tamika felt the brunt of the
struggle that came with growing up in a household exposed
to domestic violence and overwhelming poverty. She speaks
of the time her family was blacklisted on the rental property
market, finding themselves homeless until they were given a
place in a housing commission home. Recalling the weeks her

parents couldn't afford a $1 bottle of milk or $2 loaf of bread, Tamika tells of how she would meticulously scan every aisle and run her fingers along every nook and cranny in the local shopping centre, collecting 10 cent pieces, to save up for food for the following week. But the following week would come, and there would still never seem to be enough. The struggle remained the same.

Tamika tells me these early years made being a blackfulla really hard for her for a long time. It felt like her family fell into the stereotypes non-Indigenous people have of us, and she was ashamed. It wasn't until high school when Tamika participated in an Indigenous education program and got to interact with like-minded Aboriginal and Torres Strait Islander students, that she was able to realise her potential. There she would learn that she was so much more than any stereotype and came to know of the immense strength that comes with our culture.

In her early school years, though, things weren't much easier than they were within the four walls of home. Kids in class would laugh at her and tell her she was ugly, and she remembers early on one boy in particular pointing at her palm and asking her why her hand was black on one side and white on the other. When Tamika couldn't answer, he just said, 'Well you look weird anyway.'

This continued for many years, as she and her brother were the only two Indigenous kids at their school, but thankfully by the third grade a new-found passion for the ocean meant Tamika was able to distract herself from the unkind actions of her peers. It was in class that year that she first learnt about the ocean, and of the animals and ecosystems that thrived within it.

GROWING UP IN QUEENSLAND AND BEING FROM SALT WATER PEOPLE, SHE'D ALWAYS LOVED THE BEACH, BUT IT WAS FROM THAT POINT THAT SHE KNEW FOR SURE THAT ALL SHE WANTED TO BE WHEN SHE GREW UP WAS A MARINE BIOLOGIST. SHE COULD USE THE KNOWLEDGE OUR PEOPLE HAVE HELD FOR MILLENNIA TO PROTECT THE OCEAN.

She is pursuing that passion now, studying a Bachelor of Environmental and Marine Sciences with the hope of pursuing a PhD in the area in the future. As if there's not already enough on her plate, she's also working full time as a project officer at the Indigenous youth climate network Seed, which is dedicated to advocating and fighting for the protection of traditional land and waterways.

I would have had no idea of Tamika's not-so-easy start to life if she hadn't told me of it for this story. Her unrelenting positivity and kindness masks any glimmers of past trauma. She has truly turned her past experiences around, using them to fuel her continuous hard work and deep appreciation for the good in the world. You can feel the positivity and hope that Tamika carries within her, and this is particularly apparent in one of the many brilliant side projects she manages, an Instagram page called 'First Nations Affirmations'. Here she writes and shares powerful messages of hope, borne from the different elements of our culture.

**'I AM THIS LAND, INTERTWINED WITH MY SOUL. THE LAND THAT MY ANCESTORS NURTURED AND PROTECTED FOR OVER 60,000 YEARS.
CARE FOR MY COUNTRY.
CARE FOR MY ANCESTORS' SOULS.'**

To me, Tamika oozes the exact gentleness that is required as one of our leaders on the forefront of climate change advocacy. As our old people and the many thousands of ancestors before us have always done when caring for our land and waters, to successfully ensure their prosperity and health, these new leaders must tread upon country lightly, with care and caution, understanding and compassion. Tamika knows the future for us as a species now depends on how well we treat our mother Earth, how we heal her and ensure that our children and grandchildren can live within her embrace. And this is exactly why she is dedicating her life to figuring out the best way to do this.

TAMIKA'S UNDYING LOVE FOR THE OCEAN IS PERSONIFIED IN HER BEAUTIFUL SON, ILUKA. HIS NAME IS A BUNDJALUNG WORD MEANING 'BY THE SEA', AND HE HAS BECOME TAMIKA'S GREATEST INSPIRATION TO STRIVE CONTINUALLY TO BE THE BEST VERSION OF HERSELF.

Tamika pours everything she has into the many varying facets of her work. She does this because she wants Iluka's future to be one in which everyone, be they Aboriginal or not, knows and feels proud of the fact that, compared to the western world that we live in today, his culture is a peaceful, harmonious and more sustainable one.

Her wish is for non-Indigenous people to take more time to understand our people, instead of labelling and stereotyping us. She believes that if non-Indigenous people were to invest the time and effort, they would learn so much, and the world would be a better place.

With this wish, Tamika shared a letter with me that she wrote for a future Iluka, filled with all her hopes for him and what lays ahead in his life. It contains mantras, guidance and hope that I feel all of us should experience, holding these truths close ...

Dear my first born, beautiful son Iluka,

You were born to stand out my love.

As a young BLACK boy, I have and will continue to raise you to be proud of the colour of your skin.

To be proud of your unique identity as a young Aboriginal, Torres Strait and South Sea Islander boy, who will grow into the man you were destined to become.

To be proud of your culture and the ancestors that walk and guide you through this journey of life.

For you, my son, have the strength, resilience and pride of a young warrior with over 60,000 years of culture running through your veins.

Iluka, I will teach you to be impeccable with your word, speaking with integrity to use the power of your voice in the direction of truth and love.

Learn to not make assumptions, you will find the courage deep within to ask questions, for you will find the answer that you are looking for. Your education and knowledge is your greatest power, son, use the gift wisely.

Discover to not take anything personally, what others do and say is a projection of their own reality. My son, be true to who you are while always doing your best under any circumstance and NEVER let anybody silence your voice.

As your mother my wish for you is to have an honest, loving and kind heart.

As your mother my wish for you is to live a life of happiness and health.

As your mother my wish for you is to have respect for yourself and treat others the way you want to be treated.

As your mother my wish for you is to find pure, true love.

LIVE YOUR LIFE TO ITS GREATEST POTENTIAL! CHASE YOUR SWEET DREAMS!

Treat today as a gift, because we are living in the present after all.

Most of all my son, my wish for you is to know how much you are unconditionally loved by your father and I throughout this magical experience called LIFE.

Dear Iluka my baby by the sea,

Love Always your Mamma x

LET'S TALK ABOUT
CARING FOR COUNTRY

This Earth has known many stories before ours. Many thousands of feet and paws, claws and scales have swum and slithered, and jumped and run and danced across this Earth, shaping this country as they pass.

Shaping it since time began. Each heart that has beat on the soil of the great Mother, the Mother at our feet, is born from her. Belongs to her. She gives us water and brings forth food from her pores, so we may live and grow.

ALL SHE ASKS IN RETURN IS THAT ONE DAY, WHEN SHE CALLS US, WE GO HOME TO HER, THAT WE RETURN THE HEARTBEAT WE BORROWED AND FOLD OUR WEARY BONES INTO THE GROUND FROM WHERE WE CAME.

But we have exploited her. Our over-consumption, our disregard for old ways that have ensured her safety and prosperity for more than 80,000 years under Indigenous custodianship, all of it has led to her destruction and decimation.

We must heal her now. But how?

- Listen to our Indigenous leaders who know how country has always been cared for and follow their lead.

- Don't underestimate the power of individual action. Reduce your waste! Switch to reusable materials, sort your recycling and as we learnt in primary school, don't be a litterbug.

- Show up! At rallies, protests and especially when it comes to the voting booth. There is power in numbers and public pressure is key. Nothing has as great an effect on this issue than voting for the right people. Understand where different parties and people put the environment and climate change in the priority list and choose who you support wisely. Our future and our future generations depend on it.

'AS A COMMUNITY, WE ARE ALWAYS THERE FOR EACH OTHER'

SHANTELL BAILEY
WIRADJURI

I'm constantly pursuing opportunities to learn and better myself in every aspect of my life, but particularly in the areas that will benefit me in any work I do for my people. This is not only for my own growth, but, more importantly to equip myself with tools and stories that will assist in guiding those tiddas who will follow me, as they come up against the same experiences I have.

This mindset has emerged from the privilege and immeasurable advantages I've been afforded in learning from a range of incredibly wise and generous Aboriginal women over the past few years. Most of these interactions, even the ones that have lasted just a few short minutes, have had significant impacts on my understanding of self and where, as an Aboriginal woman, I belong in the world. A lot of the time I won't realise that impact, though, until I hear myself quoting one of those women and passing her lesson on to another, months or even years later.

In learning about Shantell Lee Bailey's story, a Wiradjuri woman and Legal Aid solicitor from Lithgow, New South Wales, I am aware of one of those lessons. In her line of work, Shantell has been exposed to the flaws in our legal system and has particularly noticed how the 'one size fits all' approach to justice disproportionately disadvantages Aboriginal and Torres Strait Islander people. Navigating her personal emotions and frustrations when she sees our mob suffer, while maintaining a level of professionalism and getting the job done, is a complex and emotionally taxing task.

At a former workplace of mine, where we were required to attend regular staff development days, an imposing Aboriginal woman whose voice commanded complete attention helped me put a name to the experience Shantell is facing in her work. It is an experience so many of us encounter in similar ways in different parts of our life.

This previous colleague of mine stood tall and graceful in front of a white board in the conference room we were all crammed into and drew two circles that slightly overlapped each other. Above one she wrote 'white' and above the other she wrote 'black'. Indicating that the circles represented the white world and the black world that exist in Australian society today, she then pointed to the overlapped section in the middle and said,

'THIS IS WHERE BLACKFULLAS SPEND MOST OF THEIR LIFE TODAY. IN OUR WORK, IN SOCIAL SITUATIONS AND IN THE EVERYDAY, WE'RE ALWAYS NAVIGATING BETWEEN THESE ...

What those two worlds represent is different ways of being in relation to cultural context and backgrounds. How we interact with individuals, how we react to things or the decisions we make can all be impacted by our understanding of which world a situation is coming from or of which world will be most affected by the step we choose to take.

Think of it like being at a barbecue at your white friend's house in the suburbs with all their family there. There's their dad, who you know is a Liberal Party member, and over there is their cousin, who's flaunting a southern cross tattoo on their shoulder. It's their ute parked in the driveway with the 'like it or leave it' bumper sticker that you spotted on the way in. Your 'two worlds' instincts would kick in to let you know you're very much in a white world situation, so it might not be the time to go around the room for everyone's thoughts on Treaty.

For Shantell, who works mostly with Aboriginal clients who are facing a range of civil law matters ranging from credit and debt issues to consumer law, discrimination and police complaints, even false imprisonment, there is a fine line she has to walk. It's a tightrope that extends between the black world, where she is personally invested in the emotional and political aspects of her client's treatment, and the white world of traditional western legal frameworks and protocols.

'THE BEST THING ABOUT BEING ABORIGINAL IS THE COMMUNITY. KNOWING YOU CAN GO ANYWHERE IN AUSTRALIA OR THE WORLD AND MEET ANOTHER BLACKFULLA AND YOU FEEL AT HOME.

'What makes things tough, though, is finding it hard to separate your work, which often has such a political and cultural focus, from your personal life because they are so intertwined.'

Adhering to best practice in her work while maintaining her integrity and emotional energy will largely be a process of trial and error for Shantell throughout her career. Clearly, it would be so much easier if her non-Indigenous colleagues, and the broader population, understood these circumstances better and considered how they could be more thoughtful.

Something my mob often raises is how draining it is to constantly have to 'come out', so to speak, as Aboriginal or Torres Strait Islander in new social settings and workplaces. It's a process that involves first assessing whether there's a level of cultural awareness and safety in the room. Then you'll have to consider whether you're ready to face the standard follow-up questions and justifications you'll have to dig up around your identity if you do open up. Shantell tells me she's been lucky to have mostly experienced strong workplaces where cultural competence is paramount and she has been supported, but she has also been in environments where she's left feeling overwhelmingly anxious about who she is and what colleagues think and say about her.

Another element our non-Indigenous peers and colleagues need to be aware of, which usually follows this 'outed' moment, is the presumption that we are automatically the office's endless cultural resource. Shantell acknowledges that she's studied and always worked to advocate for our communities, but she is not a one-stop-shop for all knowledge and perspectives related to Aboriginal and Torres Strait Islander matters.

There's a huge level of unpaid emotional work and engagement that Aboriginal people are continually expected to provide, whether that be in the workplace or even just among friends. Shantell finds that her friends frequently pin her as the go-to person on anything that come up on Indigenous people and culture. She's expected to contribute either a supporting or opposing argument, depending on the context, which can be so personally taxing.

When I've spoken about this before, I've found non-Indigenous people can be quite shocked by this push back. To an extent, I can understand their defensiveness, their need to assure me they just want to learn to be better allies. We're pretty good at knowing when someone is genuine and most of us really do want everyone to educate themselves so we can move forward together. It is important to understand, though, that there is a time and place, and conversations should be held with respect and consideration for the person you're asking.

A NON-TOKENISTIC WAY TO VALUE THE KNOWLEDGE OF A FRIEND OR ABORIGINAL PERSON YOU WORK WITH IS TO VIEW THE EDUCATION YOU WISH TO RECEIVE AS A PROCESS THAT TAKES TIME AND NEEDS TO TAKE PLACE ON THEIR TERMS. IT'S ABOUT OPENING THE DIALOGUE, BUILDING GENUINE CONNECTIONS AND BEING VULNERABLE AND HONEST AS TO WHY YOU WANT TO BE A PART OF THIS WITH US AND, PARTICULARLY, WHY NOW.

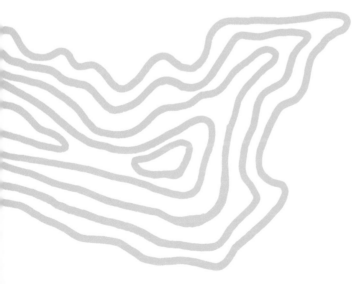

In recent years, Aboriginal people and our culture, including our art and practices, have become quite sexy to white organisations and people. This has meant there's an increasing demand to have an Aboriginal 'flavour' sprinkled over just about everything. In a lot of cases this has been to the benefit of the non-Indigenous entity involved, but not the Aboriginal person.

Avoiding compromising an individual's energy, safety and integrity can really be as simple as being willing to take your time with us. It's the only way to secure a better more harmonious and mutually beneficial future for all.

> 'I think one thing non-Indigenous people can learn from our culture is respect, humility and empathy. As a community we are always there for each other and continually help not only our own, but others too. Whether it's on the clock or not, in both our personal and professional lives.'

Ultimately, the obstacles Shantell faces in navigating two worlds are forever changing, and as uncomfortable and confusing as this can be, she assures me she will only continue to invest more blood, sweat and tears into her passion and interest in law. She will do this with every fibre of her being. Her ultimate goal is to build a bridge for our communities so they have better access to justice, a justice that is true and fair. Shantell was the first in her family to make it through university and her future is undeniably bright. Having more people like her in areas like the justice system will be a great and vital benefit to all of us. Her advice to the generation that will follow her is:

'JUST GET STARTED, JUMP IN AND FIND YOUR WAY. SOMETHING I FOUND THROUGHOUT STUDYING AND WORKING IS THAT THE MORE I DID TO FURTHER MYSELF, THE MORE I RECEIVED IN RETURN. '

'PROVIDING QUALITY EDUCATION FOR OUR NEXT GENERATION'

JESSICA ANNE FARRELL
DUNGHUTTI

If you were to ask me to list what questions I've been asked most often across my life, 'how much Aboriginal are you?', and several variations of that sentiment, would easily make up the top five. As an Aboriginal girl with a black dad and white mum, and subsequently light skin, I've found non-Indigenous people are often perplexed, almost to the point of obsession, with the audacity of my identity. As with many of my fellow brothers and sisters, I don't fit the Tourism Australia version of what an Aboriginal person looks like.

Jessica Anne Farrell, with blonde hair and blue eyes, and family ties to Dunghutti country in Kempsey, New South Wales (and therefore quite possibly another cousin of mine), would no doubt say she's spent a great deal of her life facing those kinds of questions too.

Jessica is an educator and seemed to be destined for this career from a very early age; as a little girl she would line up all her teddy bears and dolls and spend hours playing teachers and students. She'd put her auntie's hand-me-down heels on and strut around like a boss lady, keeping the toys in line, and would even create worksheets for her sisters to do too. With these imaginings now her reality, Jessica's biggest passion is providing quality education for our next generation and fighting to ensure culture is as much a part of Koori kids' school experiences as all other elements of their learning.

GROWING UP IN THE PENRITH REGION IN WESTERN SYDNEY WITH ITS HIGH POPULATION OF ABORIGINAL PEOPLE, JESSICA FOUND HERSELF STRONGLY SUPPORTED IN HER ABORIGINAL IDENTITY.

In particular, one of Jessica's aunties taught her about her culture, and at her primary school there was a strong cohort of Indigenous students, making up fifty per cent of the students at the school. She attributes part of her success and her strength and pride in her Aboriginality to that experience and believes being able to express herself as a Dunghutti girl so freely from a young age had an incredibly positive effect on her self-belief.

Once she hit high school, Jessica started to notice that being not only Aboriginal but an Aboriginal person who doesn't look how many people might expect made her stand out among her peers. Many of them had never otherwise been exposed to someone like her.

From there, standard comments such as 'what percentage Aboriginal are you?' or 'are you half or quarter?' started to rear their heads. To Jessica's greatest surprise, the disbelief in her Aboriginality even extended to statements like 'you're the prettiest Aboriginal person I've ever seen'. All of a sudden, that assured, black little bubble in which Jessica had been growing up seemed to burst.

'This made me feel as if I was second-guessing identity. I wasn't sure how to explain myself or my family history ... I also started to realise that being Aboriginal meant segregation from others. I felt lost, like a piece of me was missing.'

Since then, the constant justifications and telling and retelling of family histories to every new person she meets, not just non-Indigenous people, but at times even other Aboriginal people, hasn't stopped for Jessica. It takes its toll, especially on those days when you're left feeling like you'll never be able to prove to everyone that a burning power of incredible Aboriginal culture lives inside you; people are just too blind to see it. None of that will stop Jessica, though, she's too proud to ever stop, and she will continue telling the stories her ancestors fought to preserve. In every facet of her life she will continue to be an educator, because she knows there's so much for our non-Indigenous counterparts to learn from us.

'I BELIEVE OUR CULTURE IS CONNECTED IN A CIRCLE THAT NEVER ENDS; THERE IS NO START AND FINISH LINE LIKE IN WESTERN WAYS OF LEARNING. NON-INDIGENOUS PEOPLE WOULD BENEFIT SIMPLY FROM HAVING AN OPEN MIND ABOUT WHO WE ARE AS PEOPLE, TO SIT, TO LISTEN. OUR CULTURE ISN'T JUST ABOUT DOT PAINTINGS AND FAMOUS LAND MARKS, ITS MUCH RICHER AND DEEPER THAN THAT.'

Jessica's story is such a familiar one and as always I'm baffled, as I've never been able to understand the western obsession with using visual indicators to justify or box in an individual's identity, be it race or factors like disability, gender and sexuality. This thinking is so restricting and is in complete opposition to the nature of the human condition. For me, it is simple; human beings are fluid entities that cannot be put in boxes.

There is no one way to be woman or man; to live – be you old or young; to raise your children; to have a career; or even to live a happy life; and equally, there's no one way to look or be Aboriginal or Torres Strait Islander. We talk about the percentage questions a lot in our community, the ones so many non-Indigenous people feel compelled to ask, often with their faces scrunched up and a scratch of the head, as their eyes analyse your features.

Although the unintentional passing or unrelenting interrogation that comes with having a light skin may not be anywhere near as threatening to the safety or positive experiences of our dark-skinned mob, it is important to address how hurtful this question is – and why. It's not so much that the opinion of non-Indigenous people has such a significant impact on the strength of our identities, but more that these attitudes are so reminiscent of those that led to the Stolen Generations.

When the policies that allowed the government to steal babies from mothers' arms were imposed on our people, beginning another wave of trauma that is still being felt today, one of the guiding principles and purposes of these policies was to 'breed the Aborigine out of them'. 'Half-caste' kids, as they were referred to at the time, who came mostly from one white parent and one black, were separated from their home and their family and forced to live a 'white way' within white families. The hope was that they would have children with other white people, making their children 'less Aboriginal' and so on and so on, until eventually no connection to culture would exist for those future generations.

In asking people like me and Jessica, how much Aboriginal we are, it feels like you're asking us how much we fit in to the stereotypes you hold about our people. I get flashbacks to my high school years, when my peers followed up that question with 'what do witchety grubs taste like?' and 'did your parents get your house for free?'.

In short, connection to culture is so much more complex, rich and diverse than anyone who is non-Indigenous can understand. There's this unspoken feeling that comes with identifying as Aboriginal and being around mob that you'll never know if you aren't an Aboriginal person. Identity for us, is built on family lines, connection to country, stories, traditions and something that can't be measured according to levels of melanin.

We are all shades of colour, as my dad has always said to me, coffee is still coffee even when milk is added. Blackfullas are blackfullas no matter their colour, and nobody can speak for us and who is part of our people, except for us.

ABORIGINALITY IS LIKE COFFEE

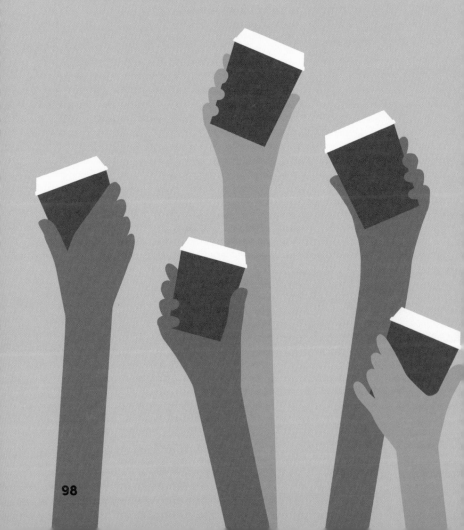

NO MATTER HOW MUCH
MILK YOU ADD,
COFFEE IS STILL COFFEE.
NO MATTER HOW LIGHT
OR DARK-SKINNED,

A BLACKFULLA
IS STILL
A BLACKFULLA

HOW MUCH TEA IS EVEN IN YA? | A POEM

By Lauren May Swain

The pot of tea has been brewing, for eighty-thousand-years long.

I'm milky, a spoon of sugar, but them blak leaves still taste strong.

Grandma's tea is blak with one, and Dad takes milk with two.

And, great, great, great Grandma has a straight-up blak-leaf brew.

Father's cup was filled on country, the land of his mothers.

A proud Wiradjuri Dabee man, eldest of his brothers.

Ancestor's tea: ancient, rich, infused on sacred ground.

Spirits heard, whispers in wind, moments untouched by sound.

Ngarigo country, my cup was poured under the peaks of snow.

Steaming with culture, yarns and songlines uncles thought I should know.

Just like father I was poured proud, happy as just me.

Until ignorant eyes questioned, 'Well how can that be?'

There's a splash too much milk, and then a spoon too much sugar!

Not black, nor brown, too white!

The tea beats within my heart and it's warm in my soul.

A tea not in part, with milk, I am tea, I am whole.

Still some say this tea is too pale, I can tell you firsthand.

But I know, that I came from that pot ...

That boiled on Dabee land.

A word from the poet ...

Aboriginality is like a cup of tea, it doesn't matter how much milk and sugar you add, it's still a cup of tea. I am a proud, milky, sugary, Wiradjuri woman brewed from the oldest pot of tea in the world. The pot that boiled on the land of the Dabee people – my people.

I was born and raised in the mountains of Ngarigo country, in the rural town of Cooma. I was lucky to grow up surrounded by my cousins, aunties and uncles on a street that rightfully earned the name 'Swain Lane'.

This poem was written for my younger self. A little girl who had been asked one too many times, 'How much Aboriginal is even in ya?' A little girl who found it easier to reserve her culture for when she was in the comfort of home, than to face the scrutiny of her skin colour. A little girl who was told she wasn't 'black enough' to be a part of her culture that she knew so strongly within her soul.

Well that little girl is no longer hiding, she's standing tall and proud. She is hopeful that other cups of tea can read this poem and stand proud, in knowing that they are BLAK enough.

'A POSITIVE AND OUTSPOKEN LEADER AND ROLE MODEL TO EVERYONE AROUND HER'

FALLON AND JORDAN HARRIS
KALKADOON AND SOUTH SEA ISLANDER

Picture this, you're a young blackfulla with a hunger to give back. More than anything, you're determined to work for and with your people, and nothing can get in your way. But it gets a bit lonely in this fight and you know there's strength in numbers, so you start looking to connect with and be supported by others just like you. Next thing you know, the universe – or your boss – answers your cries for connection and hands you an invitation to a conference, an Indigenous youth conference.

Deadly, right? What's better than being in a room full of people just like you? Just as passionate about making a change, just as energetic and creative and raring to go, and better yet, they really understand where you're coming from. They know what you've been through as an Aboriginal or Torres Strait Islander person in this day and age, because they've grown up in the same era as you and experienced the same things.

WHEN YOU GET THERE, IT'S ALL YOU COULD'VE HOPED FOR. YOU SWAP YARNS WITH YOUR FELLOW EMERGING LEADERS AND ARE IN AWE OF THE SIMILARITIES IN YOUR STORIES; IT'S LIKE YOU'VE KNOWN EACH OTHER FOR YEARS, NOT HOURS.

Then you're diving deep into discussions about solutions to some of our most complex issues. You workshop strategies, make huge plans inspired by the gleaming array of guest speakers and thought-provoking panels, and as the event flies by and nears its end, you feel pretty confident that you're going to leave it and, quite possibly, change the world.

As you're packing up to head home, you realise there's others who are just arriving. They're a bit older and the event staff have swapped out the rolls of sticker name tags and butchers' paper for 'welcome drinks' and 'goodie bags'.

This, of course, is the general conference you weren't invited too. You'll find in media coverage from the following days that while you and your new youth mates have started a Facebook group to continue building your ideas, the other conference members will close their event with joint policy proposals and ideas spoken directly to attending government ministers or the like.

It'll be a few more years before you get the same chance, and when you finally break into the big boys' and girls' auditorium, the irony will be in the guiding theme of the event: 'The Next Generation: working with Aboriginal and Torres Strait Islander young people from zero to twenty-nine'.

I've been on several 'looking to the future' or 'next generation' panels and events for young people in the past few years and, no matter the context, whether they're Aboriginal-specific or not, the flaw in each of them is relatively the same. For one hour of the day, late in the afternoon, after hours of other experts mentioning stats about youth and what they think youth need to do, one to four young representatives will emerge on stage. The crowd will 'oooh' or 'aah' as they watch us, young people with voices, opinions and expertise, as if we're unicorns. As we, the youth, stare back into the crowd, it will be obvious that we are in the minority.

The fact is, over half of all Indigenous Australians fall into the youth category. Yet there are so few of us who are praised for being in touch with the needs and attitudes of our peers on the ground, for taking initiative and building our own solutions in the areas we most care about and in which we have lived experience. We are seldom welcomed to the main stage of our national gatherings.

The overwhelming sentiment from my peers when they have found themselves in these situations is, why are we treated like an afterthought? Why are the young ones crammed into a single day, away from the sight of the older, more experienced and more powerful attendees? Why does our youthfulness seem to devalue us in the eyes of the leadership, and why is a seat at the decision- and policy-making table something that feels so out of reach?

I spoke with a Kalkadoon and South Sea Islander mum who gave me hope that just outside the 'youth' bracket an older generation exists who wants us to be heard just as badly as we do. Fallon Harris, originally from Bowen in Northern Queensland but now living on Yorta Yorta country in Victoria, has dedicated her life to bettering the experience and opportunity of community. She wants to ensure that those of us who follow her know that their voices matter and that they should feel unafraid to step up, step out and work hard for change.

Fallon works in financial literacy, assisting community to deal with issues such as gambling addiction, and particularly helping young Aboriginal women to feel empowered enough to take control of their own lives. This is her passion and she could never imagine herself working apart from mob – and why would she when they understand her, she understands them and working together means working towards a stronger and healthier community.

Fallon is now thriving as a positive and outspoken leader and role model for everyone around her. It wasn't until she was in her early thirties, though, that she realised that, like many of the Aboriginal women around her, she was being held back by her own self-doubts and struggles with mental health issues.

> *'I realised that many of my sista girls had gone through the same trauma as me. But instead of talking to each other we'd tried to deal with it the best way we could. I suffered with mental illness without reaching out, thinking I was so alone in the world. Now we are realising we are stronger together, stronger in dealing with issues together, yarning with each other.'*

THROUGH HER FEARLESSNESS IN REACHING OUT TO THOSE AROUND HER AND OPENING UP TO THEM, FALLON AND HER SISTERS HAVE DEMONSTRATED THE WAYS IN WHICH SISTERHOOD CAN NOT ONLY BRING STRENGTH AND COMPANIONSHIP, BUT HEALING TOO.

This group has found its voice. It is leading us into the future by leaning on the resilience of our mob, who, even though we still live in a world where major obstacles are thrown at us, have the strength to get back up, roll with it and never even consider quitting.

ACCORDING TO FALLON THE WOMEN AROUND HER ARE A FORCE TO BE RECKONED WITH. ONE OF THE BIGGEST AREAS ON WHICH THEY HAVE COLLABORATED AND SHARED THOUGHTS AND IDEAS IS WHAT THEY BELIEVE THEY SHOULD BE DOING IN RAISING THE NEXT GENERATION OF INDIGENOUS WARRIORS.

Fallon teaches her daughter that being a blackfulla today means that because of what those who have come before us have fought for and achieved, we each have a voice we can and should use to stand up when something is unjust.

'We need to teach our children not to be silenced, and if they feel they must speak up on issues, to do so, to find positive influences in their lives: peers, adults and role models. Who are we to silence our youth, they are our future! We need them to stand up, be proud, be aggressive in fighting for their rights – and when adults do wrong!'

Fallon and the group of like-minded women around her have passed on to Fallon's fourteen-year-old daughter Jordan a sense of the value that young voices carry. This has helped her to rise as a proud Aboriginal and South Sea Islander girl who already knows she can overcome anything, and do anything, she sets her mind to. Jordan says her mum is her biggest inspiration and although its hard growing up in a country town with a small population of other blackfullas, she's forever grateful that her mum has shown her that she can make it through anything. She knows what it means to be a proud Aboriginal woman and how great it is to be a continuation of the oldest surviving culture on Earth.

Jordan is still at high school and one day hopes to graduate and go to university. For now, though, she just wishes the non-Indigenous kids around her town, and in her school, appreciated our culture more and could begin to understand that the ways in which we've lost our old way of life continue to affect us now. She's felt lonely at times, as she's often been the only Aboriginal kid around. But thanks to her experience playing for the Rumbalara Netball Club, an all-Aboriginal run netball team, she's been able to connect with other kids just like her. It's so important to her and to her sense of belonging that she makes a seventy-kilometre return journey three days a week for two training sessions and a weekend game.

THE WAY IN WHICH JORDAN SPEAKS OF HER PRIDE IN HER CULTURE AND HER CONFIDENCE IN WHO SHE IS AS AN ABORIGINAL AND SOUTH SEA ISLANDER GIRL SHOWS CLEARLY WHAT IT MEANS TO BE RAISED BY SOMEONE WHO INSTILLS BELIEF IN THEIR CHILDREN AND VALUES WHAT THEY HAVE TO SAY.

Not only is she sure of herself, but she's also firm in what she believes to be true and important, and sees it as her duty to speak up for her people when it's not.

'I stand up for what I think is right. Especially if someone disrespects my mob or stereotypes us.'

Youth suicide, out-of-home care and juvenile detention are three major areas where we, the young blackfullas, are excessively over-represented. While we are constantly surveyed and researched in this area, why aren't we taking the lead from sisters like Fallon and ensuring that youth voices are valued and included in the development of the solutions to these major problems too?

Our older people are the core of our expertise, our knowledge holders, there's no denying that. But how can this knowledge and expertise be passed on if we're not in the room to receive it? We've been battling with a lot of the same stuff for decades and we, the babies of the group, are starting to wonder if maybe we need to try to do things a bit differently. We need to have the trust and support of the generations above us to try something new and figure out the solutions.

That's not to say we haven't been told our voices matter; we do quite often hear that in some way, shape or form, but if we aren't included in genuine, structured ways, with actual power and influence, why would we believe it?

So consider this, when next you're working on or talking about a youth issue in any context, or even planning an event: instead of thinking how 'cool' and 'fun' it would be to set up a separate, offsite youth event, what about figuring out ways to get young people, the true experts in youth, into the room.

EMBED OPPORTUNITIES FOR US TO SHARE THEIR PERSPECTIVES IN SAFE AND SUPPORTED WAYS, AND HELP US GROW TO OUR FULL POTENTIAL, ALONGSIDE YOU, AS WE STEP INTO THE LEADERSHIP ROLES OF TOMORROW.

PART III

YOU, THE FUTURE

Our future and the tiddas who will lead it is what drives me the most when I'm working on Tiddas 4 Tiddas. I am constantly striving to build it into a higher and more sturdy platform for them to leap off, as they chase dreams up into the stratosphere. It's true that each generation stands on the shoulders of those who fought before them, and in this final chapter, prepare to get a taste for how far we've come, and where we're going, through the voices of the up-and-coming leaders of tomorrow.

The future is *mine for the taking*.

(female / Indigenous / intersectional / for all)

MESSAGES FROM THE @TIDDAS4TIDDAS COMMUNITY

It's so strange for me to think of how I ended up here, writing these words for a book with my name on the front cover, all because of what started as an Instagram account. It was never intended to be more than that – a place to share the positive stories of our sisters, and for us, my sister Keely and I, to read them, have a break from the bikini model influencers or negative news stories in our social media feed, and feel good about ourselves and our mob every day.

The success we've seen now is even more incredible when you consider it's truly the collective success of every tidda who has supported us, shared their stories and championed our purpose. All those thousands of women and girls who've been our cheerleaders. They are the ones who inspire us every day and act as the best role models for the next generation in this online community.

I couldn't possibly fit all of their individual stories in these pages, even though they certainly deserve the same recognition and celebration, but I thought it was important to give at least a small insight into the wisdom and passion they hold for our success, and particularly their messages to the next generation.

We did a call out on Instagram in a simple post asking for responses to the question, 'What advice would you give the next generation of tiddas?' And within minutes, as we've come to expect from this passionate and giving community, their answers came flooding in. This is the true magic of what we've built together, a community connected online by a shared dedication to doing good and offering a hand to those who will follow us.

WHAT DO YOU WANT GIRLS TO KNOW ABOUT THE POWER YOU HOLD INSIDE YOURSELVES?

- You may be small, but your voice is mighty and your power is great.
- There's always more where that power came from!
- Your power is sometimes scary because of how massive it can be. You're amazing!
- Don't let anyone stop you – you're unstoppable.
- If men are intimidated by your power, they're not worth your time.
- You're not in competition with other females!
- Don't allow those threatened by your power to silence you.
- Love yourself first tiddas!
- The power is there even when the world refuses to acknowledge it.
- Speak up and speak out! Your voice is worth hearing!

'I JUST HOPE I CAN CONTINUE MAKING MY CULTURE PROUD'

KIRRALEE FROM KIRRAWEE
WONNARUA

Kirralee was born on Noongar country in Western Australia,
but moved back to the Sutherland Shire just south of Sydney
where both her parents grew up. She's seventeen years
old, but speaks with the certainty of someone much older.
She's blonde with blue eyes and as I ask my next question,
I know exactly the kinds of uneducated questions and
hurtful comments she's faced throughout her schooling.

> 'I've always been told by my classmates that I wasn't
> Aboriginal, because of how I look. Or I'll get side
> comments like, well if you are, you must get free uni, a
> free car, a free house and all of that. And I say to them:
> "Oh really? How's that?" I've never got anything for free.'

Her vibe is unapologetically: *Question me and my identity
all you want, I know who I am and you'll never change it.* We
met for lunch just after Kirralee had finished her second-last
high school exam. Many times throughout our conversation
I felt like I was talking to my younger self. The stories of

being the only Aboriginal female in her year at school, of having a full classroom of students turn their heads and stare when an Aboriginal story or issue is raised. Fighting for acknowledgement that the award or leadership opportunity you've been given is well deserved and not 'just because she's Aboriginal'.

Despite the many similarities, though, the distinct difference between Kirralee's story and mine is her unwavering confidence. By the time I got to the end of school, I was incredibly angry and damaged. I was too close to the trauma to be able to articulate, or even see, the resilience I possessed, whereas Kirralee is a straight-up boss.

SHE TELLS ME SHE'S GOING TO BE THE CEO OF QANTAS ONE DAY – AND I BELIEVE HER.

She tells me how she put a teacher in their place when they referred to a mixed race person as a 'halfie' and then stormed out of class. She is also matter of fact in her acknowledgement that, while it broke her heart, she made a decision to move away from one of her long-time best friends. Jealous when Kirralee became the first Aboriginal female school captain at their high school, her friend had stooped to disrespecting her and her culture. As she shares these aspects of her story so far, I know they come from a place of strength and self-assuredness. It took me six years longer than Kirralee to arrive at the place she's at.

Just like Kirralee, I was born and raised on Dharrawal country in the Sutherland Shire, and my old high school is just a few kilometres from hers. The area is naturally beautiful and it's been a privilege to grow up so close to the beach. What the area is most widely known for, though, is the landing of Cook on the Kurnell peninsula and the infamous race riots of the early 2000s.

For a long time my younger sister and I were the only two kids who identified as Koori at our high school and this made for a tough environment to grow up in. Plenty of misconceptions, misunderstandings and blatant xenophobia were thrown in our faces by peers and even teachers. Often, it seemed they were all trying their best to devalue our identity and pride – trying to convince us that even if we were Aboriginal, which they often refuted, there was nothing good about that anyway.

In all honesty, this has built up a bitterness within me towards this part of the world. I constantly fear for kids like me who are going to school in 'the Shire' now. In my day I had to endure 'Marlee Silva sniffs petrol' being graffitied all over school property. With the introduction of social media and online bullying, who knows what the mean and insecure kids would be able to do to young, vulnerable blackfullas now?

IT IS A NEVER-ENDING SOURCE OF INSPIRATION AND JOY TO LEARN ABOUT ALL THE AMAZING EMERGING INDIGENOUS GIRLS ACROSS THE COUNTRY – AND I GET TO DO THIS EVERY DAY WITH THE TIDDAS 4 TIDDAS COMMUNITY. BUT I CAN'T DENY THAT THERE'S SOMETHING PARTICULARLY SPECIAL IN FINDING YOUNG WOMEN WHOSE STORIES SOUND A LOT LIKE MY OWN.

I can't tell you how much Kirralee's story and presence excites me. It tells me that I don't have to hold such great fears for Koori kids in the Shire and other areas across the country that have a low Aboriginal population. Yes, unfortunately it is obvious that our young ones are still forced to face the things we have in the past, and there's a way to go, but it's definitely getting better.

Kirralee talks about an amazing non-Indigenous teacher who's committed to ensuring all the Aboriginal kids in the school feel connected to each other; he's doing this by hosting a yarning circle with them on a weekly basis. As the broader population becomes more educated about our situation and what we need as a people, support systems, like those within schools, will improve. NAIDOC and Reconciliation Week celebrations also give kids more opportunities to express themselves and their culture. I have found that Kirralee feels less alone than I did and this truly gives me so much hope.

To sum it all up, she talks to me about the future and the hopes she holds for it:

'I JUST HOPE I CAN CONTINUE MAKING MY CULTURE PROUD JUST AS MUCH AS I AM PROUD TO BE A STRONG ...

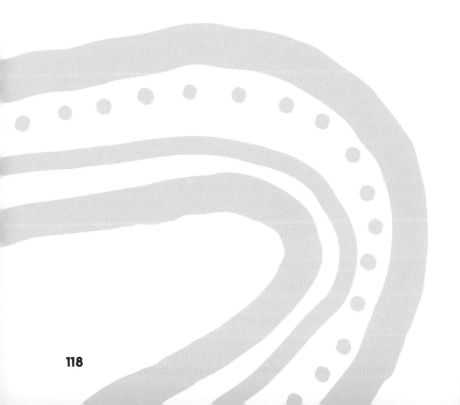

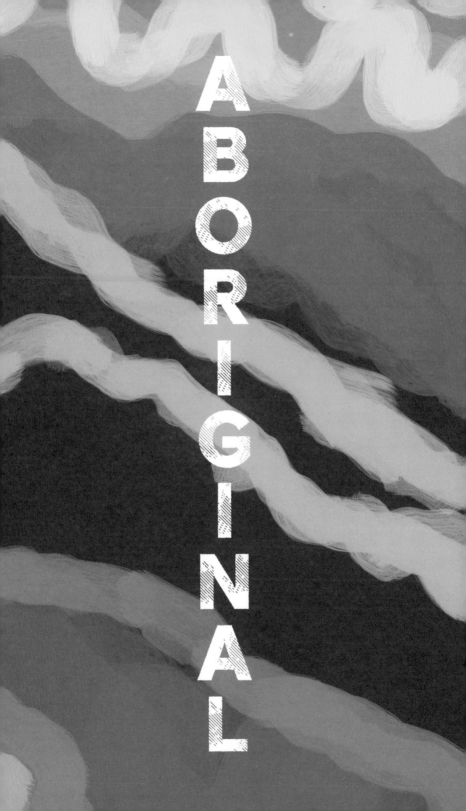

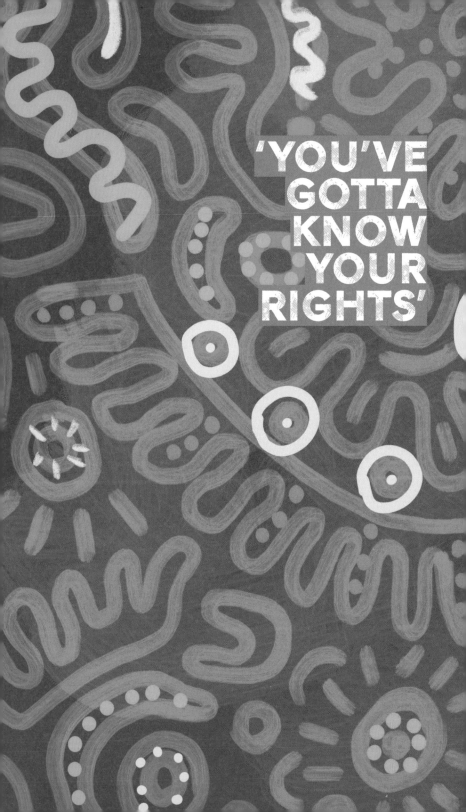

'YOU'VE GOTTA KNOW YOUR RIGHTS'

ASHLEIGH AND MADDY BRIDGE
WIRADJURI

Trigger warning: Assault, domestic violence, suicide.

Having been introduced to the legal system as a victim or crime at a very young age, nineteen-year-old Ashleigh Bridge is more personally invested in pursuing a law degree than most.

She tells me of how she was attacked by a man on her way home from school when she was just seven years old. In the immediate aftermath, her mind blocked out a lot of the details, but the event left deep wounds that had terrifying consequences later in life.

Ten years after this event took place, just as she was finishing high school, the stress of exams triggered a flood of memories; when these came rushing back, they sent her into a deep depression. At its peak, the trauma pushed her to make an attempt at ending her own life.

When I speak to her over the phone, she is matter of fact in her tone and speaks with an articulation and honesty far beyond her years. I can tell she is keen to share her past so she can help others and once again I'm blown away by the resilience and unwavering sense of duty to give back that all of our women seem to hold.

I am heartbroken for Ashleigh, and what she's been through, but as we speak she emphasises how lucky she feels to have survived it all. She tells me of the things she feels she needs to do in her life now, and I am hopeful and so proud of her. 'I need to make the most out of it', she says.

To Ashleigh, making the most of it means fighting on the ground, protesting for what she believes in. It was when she started participating in protests that she really started to think about her rights as a protestor, as a citizen and as an Aboriginal woman. This ignited a passion to represent our people and support them in the legal system, to make sure these rights are respected. Her pride in her Aboriginality, her culture and its power is the driving force for all she does. It means everything to her, it is her whole identity – and it has given her resilience, a strong connection to community and a deep sense of who she is and her purpose in life. Her self-assuredness is something her peers have previously envied, particularly as they were finishing high school and discussing the steps that would follow in the real world.

'WHEN I GRADUATED FROM SCHOOL I REALISED THE STRENGTH IN WHAT BEING ABORIGINAL HAD GIVEN ME, OVER MY FRIENDS. WHILE THEY WERE ALL LIKE, "I DON'T KNOW WHO I AM. I DON'T KNOW WHAT I'M GOING TO DO." IT WASN'T REALLY A QUESTION FOR ME, I ALWAYS KNEW WHAT I WANTED TO BE AND WHO I WAS.'

Ashleigh knows there's so much that non-Indigenous people can learn from us, from our ways of being. Whether it's the way we communicate and work with other people in community, whom we treat as family (whether they're actually related or not), or our inherent ability to leave our egos at the door. The realness and rawness of being a blackfulla is not something you see very often outside our mob.

WE LEAD WITH OUR HEARTS AND PUT CARE AND KINDNESS FIRST, AND HAVING MORE OF THESE TWO ELEMENTS OF HUMANNESS IS SOMETHING ALL CORNERS OF THE GLOBE WILL BENEFIT FROM.

When it comes to building a better nation for all those who live in it, we need to understand each other better. Aboriginal and Torres Strait Islander people only make up three per cent of the Australian population; we want the other ninety-seven per cent of the population to feel pride in our culture and our stories too, to walk with us and pave a brighter future for the next generation.

One of the major barriers to being successful in this is the fear of getting things wrong, of causing offense when trying to start conversations. But there is no shame in making mistakes; we all have room to learn and grow, and the fear of falling on your face shouldn't stop you from taking the first step. As Ashleigh puts it:

> 'I think people are scared to ask questions, and that's doing so much of a disservice, because a lack of communication is dangerous ... if an Aboriginal person says, this is the way it is. Say, "Okay, thank you for informing me." Don't say, "Oh, I'm sorry." Because that forces the person to say, "Oh, no, it's okay." Because it's not okay. Say thank you. Thank you for educating me.'

Though I may only be six years older than Ashleigh, I find myself thinking about her story, and the lessons she has to share, and how in awe I am of the way she speaks at such a young age. I never doubt the power of a young person to advocate for change and to make it happen. My favourite saying has always been *A baby shark is still a shark*. When I think of Ashleigh and the growing number of powerful, assured young activists she is a part of, I see them as having this same power and fearlessness. These young activists are emerging to speak up on a range of issues all across the country. What are the ingredients at play in this groundswell of action? When we see more and more young people at protests, or in the case of the School Strike 4 Climate, organising them, how can the older generations say this young generation is too lazy and obsessed with their phones to do anything?

In our conversation, Ashleigh reminds me of what has happened in the outside world during her years of schooling to help shape her as a natural-born activist. She names the Black Lives Matter movement that first arose in the United States, and the same-sex marriage plebiscite in Australia. And the tragic death of Elijah Doherty, a teenage Aboriginal boy from Kalgoorlie in Western Australia who died at the hands of a white farmer, bringing the issue of race relations in the town boiling to the surface. In the face of these pivotal events it makes such sense to me that Ashleigh was so stirred to take action.

In the case of *Black Lives Matter*, the rise of the movement marked a change in the way we think about what it means to protest and who can be an activist. It revealed the power of social media as a democratic and accessible forum in which everyone can participate to become a catalyst for what goes viral. The debate that surrounded the same-sex marriage plebiscite in Australia signified a major paradigm shift towards progressive change, inclusion and equality. It was one of the most significant rulings in our lifetime and emphasised the power people can have, reassuring us that things don't have to remain as they always have been.

When it comes to the story of young Elijah, the impact it had on our community was one of sheer devastation. Ashleigh remembers breaking down in class one day just after it happened:

> 'I think I had a sense of survivor's guilt ... I had a lot of family back in Cowra and Dubbo [New South Wales] and I was living this life where I wasn't in harm's way and I felt like I just left them behind.'

Seeing the face of Elijah all over social media left most of us thinking that it could've been any one of our brothers, nephews, sons or grandsons. It reminded us of how far we still need to travel to become a truly united nation.

At the age Ashleigh is now, I had a similar moment of forced realisation when the Adam Goodes media storm of 2013 erupted after he spoke out against racism. It was a defining moment for my understanding of what it means to be black in Australia today.

IN MY HOUSEHOLD, BEING ABORIGINAL WAS THE GREATEST THING YOU COULD BE AND MY FAMILY AND I WATCHED ADAM STAND UP STRONG, BURSTING WITH PRIDE. IN THE SAFETY OF OUR FOUR WALLS, OUR BLACKNESS WAS SOMETHING ALL OF US COULD BE PROUD OF, BUT OUTSIDE, THE VERY OPPOSITE MESSAGE WAS BEING GIVEN.

My peers at school called him 'weak', saying he wasn't 'a man' for becoming 'emotional like that'. At the heart of it, they couldn't understand the racial connotations in calling someone an ape. Similarly when it came to Elijah, many outside our community called him a 'troublemaker' or a 'criminal' who 'got himself in to trouble'. They seemed to think he'd decided his own fate.

These moments, of which there are far too many, have been so disheartening. At times they have left us feeling as if Australia has lied to us about its acceptance and understanding of who we are as a people. In disregarding Adam's emotions, in denying the injustice Elijah and his family face, our right to feel safe and our need to fight for this safety has been disregarded too.

But you see, while that hurts and weighs heavily on us, there is solace for us in the following knowledge:

PRESSURE MAKES DIAMONDS AND ADVERSITY MAKES ...

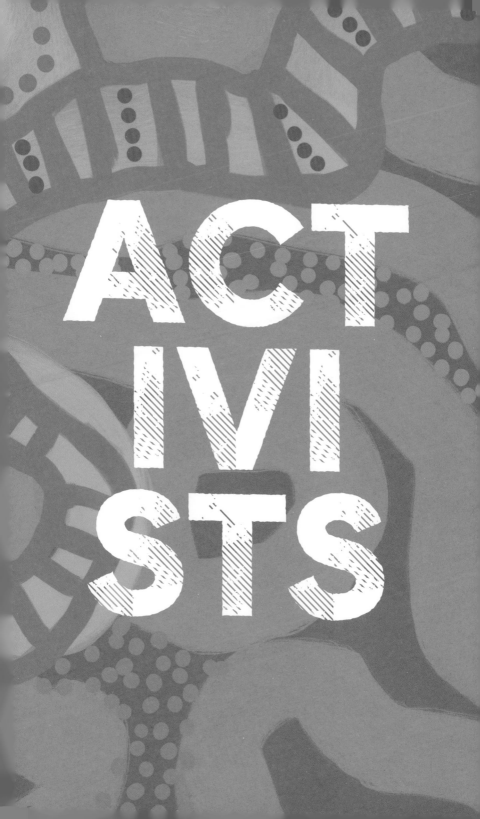

ACT
IVI
STS

When asked who her biggest role model is, Ashleigh told me it has always been her older sister Maddy. Maddy, who is only three years older than she is, stepped up into a parent role, as their Mum was chronically ill for a lot of their childhood. I spoke to Maddy next and she told me that they've always been a rock to each other; they've both seen hardship in different stages of their lives and made it through, thanks to the support they've received from each other.

Maddy will be the first in their family to graduate from university, when she completes her Bachelor of Social Work, an area of study about which she is particularly passionate. Like Ashleigh, she has been personally affected by social issues and in her case this includes domestic violence.

In her early years of university, Maddy thought she'd met the love of her life, a young black man with the same passion for working with community that she had. At first, it seemed perfect; her family loved him and the two of them were supporting each other to get through their studies smoothly.

However, things changed a few months in, with Maddy starting to see dangerous signs in her partner's behaviour.

> *'I started seeing red flags that I didn't realise at the time would be the beginning of the abuse I would experience for two years. I naively believed that if you're dating someone, and you love them, that you wouldn't do anything on purpose to hurt each other, but I learnt otherwise.'*

Abuse and controlling behaviours increasingly dominated their relationship. It even got to the point where Maddy's partner stopped her from leaving his house to go to her own home for a few nights.

A lot of people ask Maddy why she didn't leave him sooner than she did. It's a conversation she finds really difficult to have. She explains the main hesitation she had about leaving was having to reveal that she was doing so because of abuse. She didn't want to be the one who has led to an Aboriginal man with a promising potential career failing to achieve his goals. She thought it was her responsibility as an Indigenous woman to heal him, as she knew his violence was born from his own trauma and pain.

A year and a half into this tragic and unimaginably difficult experience, Maddy found the strength to put herself first and approached a counsellor at university. She was feeling increasingly unsafe, had watched her grades drop, was experiencing a decline in her mental health and had lost contact with a lot of family and friends. The counsellor put her in touch with a women's domestic violence service and she was assigned an Aboriginal caseworker. Maddy says that this caseworker changed her life, reminding her of her worth and emphasising that Maddy's life and future mattered.

Now that Maddy is safely out of the toxic relationship she was in, she focuses on the silver lining she has been able to find in this experience, which is her ability to relate to clients in her social work.

> 'I now have a greater understanding of the gaps within the system for Indigenous women experiencing domestic or family violence. I'm committed to helping Indigenous women and children, and doing everything I possibly can to ensure they are heard, and that they are supported.'

Maddy dreams that one day, with the support of local Elders in the Western Sydney community, she will open her own service for Indigenous women and children who are experiencing violence. She wants to provide a safe space for our women, where they feel supported and are able to access culturally appropriate services in community. Time and time again when our people are faced with trauma and tough times, this is how they respond: by dedicating themselves to ensuring others going through the same thing will have more support and not have to go it alone.

Maddy's advice to other females is simply to know your worth and believe in yourself; it's advice that she wishes she'd given to herself at a younger age.

> *'I know it's a super cliché but when I was younger I let others define me, and set low expectations of what I could accomplish, because most of the time people (usually non-Indigenous people) just saw me as a blackfulla from Western Sydney. But being a blackfulla from Western Sydney is actually my greatest asset and gives my life purpose, and I just wish I knew that when I was younger!'*

STRENGTH AND DETERMINATION IN THE FACE OF ADVERSITY RUNS SO STRONG IN THE BRIDGE BLOODLINE.

The clear determination these two sisters have shown in spite of what they have had to overcome within their early lives foreshadows for me two beacons of influential leadership and positive changemaking. The stories these young women have shared with me have taught me so much, and I'm sure there are many others who will learn from them. I feel so incredibly proud of them both. These women truly are our future and it is a bright one.

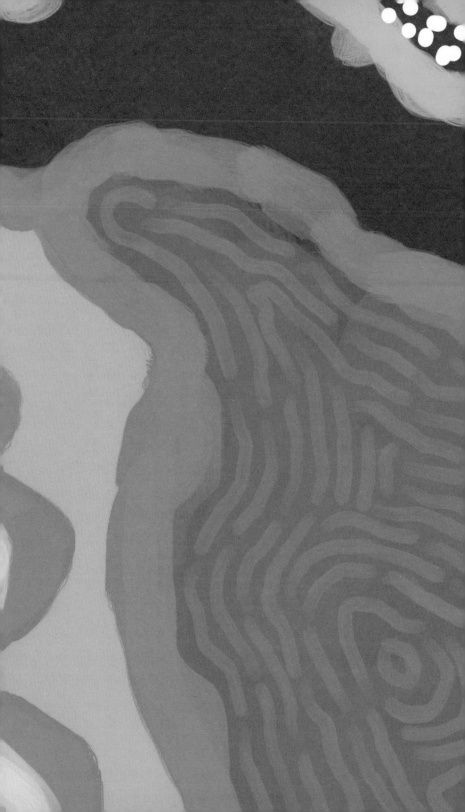

'YOU JUST HAVE TO BE STRONG AND UNAFRAID TO BE WHO YOU ARE, OR WHO YOU WANT TO BE.'

LAKOTA MORRIS
KOORI

Social media can be a scary place for a teenage girl. Opening an app like Instagram can feel like diving into a sea of constructed, perfect lives, where one is confronted with unrealistic body images and a whole lot of pressure to be, look and act a certain way. It's encouraging to see trends like those promoted by body-positive influencers emerging. *#realtalk*-style posts that reveal the realities of life online and off are becoming more common, but the faces behind these posts remain predominantly white. Often they don't really speak to our young tiddas and other black and brown girls.

When apps and celebrities on social media dictate so much of our popular culture, the trends and attitudes on issues and movements, who does an Aboriginal or Torres Strait Islander girl look to? We've tried to answer this with the Tiddas 4 Tiddas page and podcast, but none of it would be successful if it weren't for the plethora of women and girls who are walking the walk every day. Gamilaroi and Barkindji girl Lakota Morris is a perfect example of this.

One morning, in the early days of Tiddas 4 Tiddas, in among my own Instagram scrolling – and undeniably the comparisons I was making between my life and those I follow on social media – a striking Koori model caught my eye. She was wearing an Aboriginal-designed swimsuit, and I'd never seen her before. In this particular shoot, Lakota spoke of her dreams to become an international model, inspired by the likes of Samantha Harris. She wanted to have her face everywhere, to show other tiddas that they could do it too and to act as a rebuttal to a comment she received all too often from non-Indigenous people: 'You're too pretty to be Aboriginal.'

I could tell she was young, but she had the poise of a seasoned professional. I was so enthralled by her face and words that it wasn't until I went onto her personal profile to read more about her story and then looked back at the picture that I noticed a long scar stretching from her belly button up towards her sternum. Just a few weeks before she turned sixteen, Lakota was dealt the kind of news most of us fear ever hearing: she had cancer. It was a rare type of cancer called cystic mesothelioma inclusion and it had caused tumours to grow along her abdomen. Soon after that upcoming birthday, she'd need to have major surgery to remove them and that's where she would get the scar. From then on, it would act as a daily reminder not only of what she's been through, but also what she's capable of surviving.

FAST-FORWARD TWO YEARS AND NOT ONLY IS LAKOTA CANCER FREE, SHE'S FOUND A WAY TO TURN AROUND THE TRAUMA OF A SCARY DIAGNOSIS AND THE INTENSE MEDICAL PROCEDURES THAT FOLLOWED. IT HAS LED TO HER PASSION AND DETERMINATION TO EMERGE AS A PROUD ADVOCATE FOR CULTURE, THE STRONG REPRESENTATION OF ABORIGINAL PEOPLE, ANTI-BULLYING AND POSITIVE BODY IMAGE.

Lakota got into modelling before she became sick so she could beat the stereotypes of what it means to be Indigenous and successful. She wanted to overcome the self-doubt and sadness that came with the relentless bullying she faced from her peers at school. But going back to the world of modelling after facing such an enormous change in her body made her hesitate. As teenagers, we're fighting to get to know our body as hormones and puberty bring about so many changes; throwing a major illness into the mix must be even more confusing and complex.

When I spoke to her, she told me that when she was battling cancer, she didn't know if she'd ever model again. She feared her body would never work the same and she'd stop being offered work. That shoot I saw her in was her first one back in the game; not only was she able to prove the bullies who'd tried to hold her back at school wrong, she was also able to allay any of her own doubts and fears. An even more positive result was saying no when the photographer that day had offered to Photoshop the scar out in the final images. She liked how it looked, that it told her whole story; after making it through what she has, how could Lakota be scared of what anyone thought of her and her looks? Lakota is a warrior – her scar and her attitude are both testaments to that.

Lakota no longer wants to be a full-time model; she feels she can make a greater difference working as a police officer, building better relationships between the police force and our community – and we all know she's more than tough enough to do that work.

WHATEVER LAKOTA ENDS UP DOING, NOTHING WILL STOP HER FROM BEING AN INSPIRATION TO THOSE AROUND HER, FROM BEING A ROLE MODEL FOR THE GENERATION OF ABORIGINAL GIRLS THAT WILL FOLLOW HER.

She uses her online presence to share her own story, the lessons it has taught her and the big hopes she holds for the future. In a recent post she addressed the bullying she has encountered in the past and the negativity she's faced in life so far:

'Growing up being a Koori girl wasn't easy. It still isn't easy. I had a dream once upon a time to be a model. Not just any model but an Indigenous model from Australia. To show my people that if I can do it, so can you. I was bullied through primary school and high school, I've had battles that no one should ever have to go through. My dream was crushed by those haters:

"Your negativity used to hold me down in some bubble that wouldn't pop. Well I popped that bubble a long time ago. Now do you see what I'm capable of? I went through cancer at the age of 16 and still do photoshoots, I did a damn swimsuit photoshoot that I did not think I was capable of. Not only did I prove the haters wrong, I proved myself wrong. All their lies and hurtful things became my truth. I believed every bad thing that was said about me. I have grown into a young woman who isn't very confident but confident enough to share my story!

I will NOT let your lies and negativity get the best of me EVER again. Do you hear me?! Good. Because you'll see me on tv, watching me being the best I can be. I'm here for myself. You have made me who I am today, I am no longer weak, I am Me. A strong ass independent female from the Gamilaroi and Barkindji nations!

"I love the support I get from everyone, I know I don't have many followers but it's not about the followers, it's about who I am and my dreams, you don't gotta have 50 million follows just to be heard. You just have to be strong and not afraid to be who you are or who you want to be."'

When I wonder who are the ones that speak to our young women and girls on social media, what I find most exciting is that it is young leaders like Lakota. It's tiddas who have profiles and use them because they are committed to honesty and truth instead of trying to paint a picture of a perfect life.

THEY ARE DEDICATED TO LIFTING OTHER FEMALES UP, TO SHOWING THAT BEAUTY COMES IN ALL FORMS, NOT JUST ONE COLOUR OR SHAPE. THEY SHARE STORIES OF SURVIVAL AND TRIUMPH AND THEY OPEN THEIR ARMS TO THEIR ONLINE COMMUNITIES WITH BRAVE WORDS THAT REVEAL THEIR VULNERABILITY AND PUT OUR SMALL WORRIES INTO PERSPECTIVE, REMINDING US THAT IT'S ALL GOING TO BE OKAY.

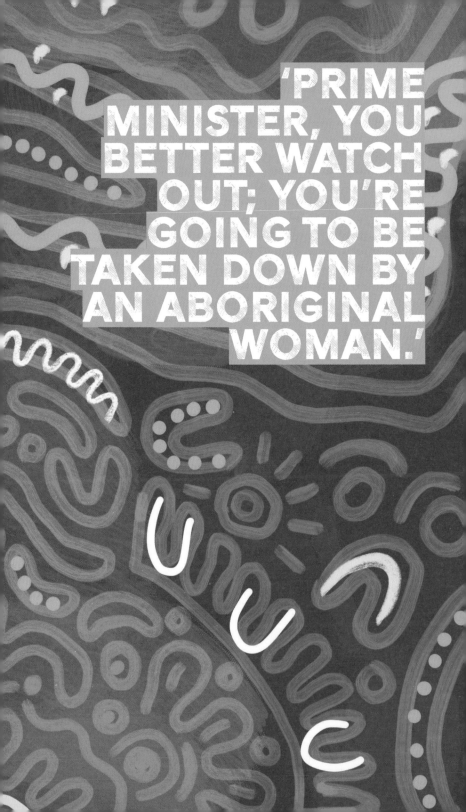

STELLA AHKIT BURGOYNE
MIRNING AND KOKATHA

In my interviews for this book, I have asked each woman and girl to tell me what they'd change if they were the prime minister of Australia. I guess I originally thought this was a way for us to begin imagining an idyllic future Australia. One where all would prosper under the leadership of a black woman whose name we'd definitely know, who wouldn't get knifed by her fellow party members. We would burst with pride every time she appeared on screen, just as I feel now whenever I hear about our Kiwi neighbour's current Prime Minister, Jacinta Ardern.

Nearly all of the tiddas I spoke to responded with some variation of: 'That's a huge question because there's so much that needs to change.' This was then followed by an extensive list of complex matters they'd wish to address, which only served to reflect my own naivety back at me. In hindsight, it is obvious that the road to the brightest future we hope for is a complex one that will take many years and, quite possibly, many consecutive black leaders to reach. A more important question to lead this particular conversation, I would suggest, is not what would you do as prime minister, but how do we get you there in the first place?

In early 2019 the ABC released a documentary called *Will Australia ever have a black prime minister?* It posed the question of how likely it was that an Indigenous Australian born today would one day become the leader of our nation. Unfortunately, the statistical analysis didn't produce the promising outcome we hoped for, with the results showing the odds are around one in six million for our mob to get there. For starters, it was suggested, the socio-economic factors relating to Indigenous opportunities and the 'Closing the Gap' targets the government has set would have to be significantly progressed for these odds to be reduced.

If that really is the case, the sad truth is, nobody knows how long it would take. Especially when as a country we are so used to leaders who fail to make much change in any area let alone that which relates to us. Truly good, reliable or significant leadership on any side or level of Australian politics seems to be sadly lacking. In so many cases the issues that impact us the most, from youth suicide to the impact of climate change on our traditional lands and waterways, simply can't continue to be put off.

To be honest, when my mind gets deep into these kinds of topics, I end up feeling a little hopeless. It suddenly seems so audacious to believe that there will be a black prime minister in my lifetime or even my children's. But right when this hopelessness begins to feel overwhelming and I'm ready to give up on that dream, I'm reminded that thankfully I live the type of life where I get to meet deadly young women like Stella.

Stella Ahkit Burgoyne, high school student and Mirning and Kokatha girl from Port Lincoln in South Australia, has an unfaltering vision for the future. At just seventeen, she has emerged as a prominent voice in the School Strike 4 Climate movement in her state, she has presented her arguments on why Aboriginal studies should be compulsory for all students to the South Australian Board of Education and uses her personal social media presence as a platform for educating her peers about Aboriginal culture and advocating for our rights. Stella has unequivocally made up her mind about where she wants to be in the future, and that is Parliament House.

How is she so sure that's where she'll end up? She's recognised it as inevitable, given the more than eighty thousand years of anecdotal evidence that Aboriginal and Torres Strait Islander culture has provided us with the tools and expertise to lead and make sustainable, positive change:

'WE'RE THE OLDEST CONTINUOUS SURVIVING CULTURE IN THE WORLD, IT DOESN'T GET BETTER THAN THAT.'

Stella concedes that she hasn't always been this confident. Both her mum and dad have always been incredibly proud role models for. They've both worked in various Aboriginal sectors and committed their lives to their community, but in her early teenage years she hadn't yet found her own voice, to be able to raise it with theirs.

It was only when Stella attended an all Indigenous netball academy with a group of like-minded Aboriginal and Torres Strait Islander girls from all over the country that she was given the opportunity to fearlessly be herself. She gained the strength to explore new ways to represent her people and to fight for and alongside them. Stella describes how being in a room full of tiddas who had the same background, stories, worries and feelings as her own made her feel that she truly belonged:

'IT WAS LIKE I WAS FINALLY ...

As one of the younger girls in the academy, she found so much strength in the leadership of the older ones; they empowered her by letting her know that her voice mattered and that she should use it. Stella's story feels so similar to my own; those older sister girls at the Indigenous youth leadership camp I went to when I was around Stella's age opened their arms wide to me. This emphasises the responsibility we all have at every stage of life to be role models to the younger ones who look up to us. Whether it's your siblings, your cousins or a tidda you meet briefly at a school event, you never know who is watching you and learning through your actions and attitudes what it means to be a blackfulla.

Stella tells me that other Aboriginal girls are coming to her for guidance and they have let her know what her strength means to them. She recently had a tidda she'd never met reach out to her on Instagram to thank her for her posts, and to let Stella know that she had given her confidence in her Aboriginality. This tidda had never felt accepted before because of her light skin.

To me this is a testament to the women and girls who are standing with their heads tall, knowing that to be a blackfulla

is to be successful. They understand that the power they hold within themselves gives others the strength to follow their lead.

As she continues her development as a leader and takes more and more steps towards the highest point of leadership in the land, Stella wants other girls to know they need to support each other; she wants them to be happy for their fellow sisters when they succeed; that's how females will continue to rise. As for the current government, Stella has a stern warning for current Prime Minister Scott Morrison: 'Prime Minister, you better watch out: you're going to be taken down by an Aboriginal woman.'

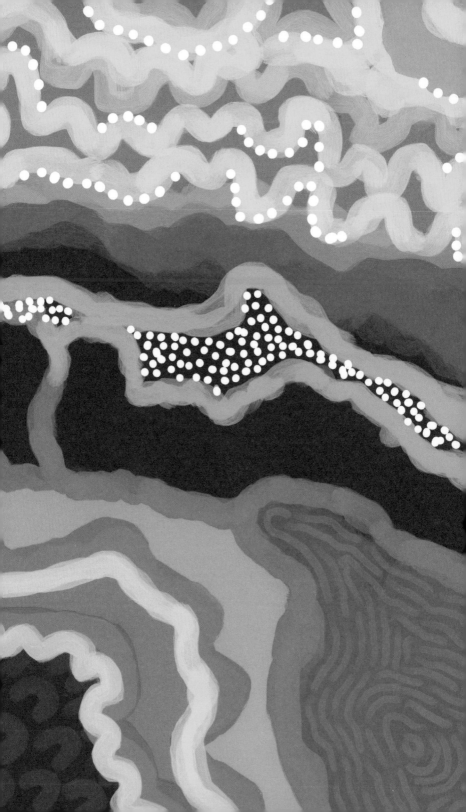

MY DEAR TIDDAS AND SISTERS

CONCLUSION

It's been almost a decade since that first plane trip I took
without my parents to a leadership camp on the Gold Coast.
Almost a decade since my shoulders straightened, making me
stand tall, with those questions 'who's your mob?' and 'where
are you from?'; by those brave voices of the young women
around me; by the permission they gave me to be proud and
loud; by those first moments in which I was submerged in the
power of the sisterhood.

In February 2020, when I'd finished all my interviews with the
immeasurably generous, kind and inspirational tiddas who
make up this book, I found myself back where it all began. Up
on Yugambeh country, in the very stadium where I spent my
final night of that defining camp back in 2011. The nostalgia
was heavy, and the immense expression of cultural pride
surrounding the Indigenous All Stars rugby league event
that had brought us there left me highly emotional. My sister
had been called up to a representative touch football team

that played the curtain raiser game before the main event. Both my parents and a few of our closest friends had joined us there to celebrate. Soon after the final whistle of her game (a disappointing loss), and cushioned by the love and respect shared between her teammates and their Maori opposition, a crowd of high school–age students adorning matching shirts and buzzing with hormones flooded in to the rows adjacent to us.

I recognised who they were immediately. As I watched the group, I noted that their shirts were way cooler than the simple white polos we'd worn back in the day, and that far more of them had iPhones in hand. But these young brothers and sisters – waving their flags, cheering loudly and singing songs that had new meaning thanks to the memories that had been made throughout the previous week, even trying their best to ignite a 'Mexican wave' with the rest of the crowd – were exactly like I had been just nine years earlier. I was overjoyed to see the camp was still running and spun around to Mum in the seat next to me. I was recalling my stories from that special time, laughing about my side fringe and commenting on the weird paradox of that it felt so long ago, yet the time had passed so fast, when suddenly I felt a tap on my shoulder.

I TURNED TO FIND THREE YOUNG SISTER GIRLS NERVOUSLY SMILING DOWN AT ME IN MY SEAT. I STOOD TO MEET THEIR GAZE AND OFFERED THEM A HELLO, QUICKLY TRYING TO SCAN MY BRAIN FOR THEIR NAMES IN CASE I'D MET THEM BEFORE. THEN ONE OF THEM ASKED, 'ARE YOU MARLEE SILVA, FROM TIDDAS 4 TIDDAS?'

It took me a moment, but I laughed back in mild disbelief. Yes, they were right. That's me.

They told me they just wanted to come and say how much they love the Instagram page, how the stories made them feel good, made them excited to be blackfullas, and they wondered if I'd mind having a picture taken with them. Of course I didn't mind; in fact, I was honoured. I told them I was an *All Stars* kid too, back in its first year, and asked them how they had found it, 'it's been the best week of my life,' one of them said. And there it was: the full circle.

I had a pic taken with the girls, hugged them goodbye and wished them fun on their final night. I then rushed back to my seat and with shaking hands fumbled to get my sunglasses back on before they could tell I was crying.

I really had just been approached by my fifteen-year-old self. I could see her at the peak of her pride, her sense of belonging clearly on display as she beamed up at me, telling *me* that what I do now means so much to her. For that moment it all felt too much for me. There was the immensity of my own growth, and, accompanying that, the memories of everything I had gone through at that age. I felt the weight of all the times I hadn't felt that good about who I was, and what that meant. Alongside that, though, was the immense pride I felt in hearing that the things you pour yourself into every day really are having an impact.

For a lot of women, but particularly women of colour or other minority backgrounds, imposter syndrome is something they face every day when they find success in what they do, or step out from the expectations broader society has of them. It refers to an overwhelming sense that you don't deserve to receive recognition or praise or to have the opportunities you've received or be on particular platforms. It can feel like you've stumbled into the wrong room and the people there have mistaken you for someone else, and that this is why you've been given the space, not because of your hard work or skill.

My own personal imposter syndrome and I have a long-standing relationship. I know exactly what triggers her appearance, and we're still working on that, but I'm getting better at pushing her aside so that I can accept praise and truly believe I deserve the privileges I have. She perked up loud and clear when those lovely tiddas came up to me at the football, and she's been hanging around quite a bit throughout the process of writing this book.

Why do these women want to tell me their story? Why do they trust me? I'm nobody.

It's all just some crazy dream or fluke; tomorrow I'll wake up back in reality.

This isn't meant to be for me, it's for someone else. They've got the wrong tidda.

Each of those thoughts has crossed my mind, but in moments of clarity I realise this is unfair. On a fundamental level, I know why I am here on this Earth at this point in time. I know what my grandmothers and my ancestors have laid out for me on my path. To question their knowledge and foresight is arrogant. All I've ever done and will ever do is tell stories.

The stories you've just read, aren't about me, nor are they even exclusively Aboriginal and Torres Strait Islander women, they're about all of us.

THESE STORIES ARE ABOUT THE ULTIMATE STRENGTH OF SISTERHOOD, COMMUNITY AND RESILIENCE, ABOUT THE IMPORTANCE OF ALL OF US SEEING AND CELEBRATING EACH OTHER'S TRIUMPHS.

I hope they have pushed you to think differently; I hope they've taught you something about the beauty and excellence of the founding culture of this continent now known as Australia; and most of all I hope that in the days when things are less bright, they can be something you come back to, to remember your own power and your ability to overcome adversity.

My dear tiddas and sisters,

I thought of you today – like every day.
I thought of your magic, your charm and your wit.
I thought of how you think of me,
how we think of us, how we think of it.

It, our place in this world I mean.
This world where we, with wombs and breasts,
often go unheard – unseen.

But, my dear tiddas and sisters,
if you've got me and I've got you,
like our aunties and grandmums paved the path for us,
we've got this next step too.

When it next gets tough – and we know it will –
please know, however far apart we may seem,
we're right beside you, armed and at the ready,

Just as we always have been.

FURTHER READING, WATCHING AND FOLLOWING

Want to know more about something raised in this book or to keep up to date on things happening in our communities? Use this list as a starting point for immersing yourself more into our culture and current affairs. This isn't an exhaustive list by any means, but it's a great place to start.

WHAT TO READ

- *Dark Emu*, **Bruce Pascoe (Magabala Books, 2014).** Arguably the most important book published that draws on historic and scientific information to reveal Indigenous knowledge and practices prior to invasion, pieced together from accounts drawn from the diaries of the first colonisers.

- *Growing Up Aboriginal in Australia*, **edited by Anita Heiss (Black Inc, 2018).** A biased recommendation, admittedly. My first published work, a short story called 'Cronulla to Papunya', is included in this anthology. But it is among an incredibly diverse and comprehensive collection of different Aboriginal voices, telling of their experiences growing up in Australia.

- *Swallow the Air*, **Tara June Winch (UQP, 2006).** This novel inspired me to be a writer and speaks to growing up as a young black woman who finds her identity so poignantly.

- **'The Australian Dream: Blood, History and Becoming', Stan Grant (Quarterly Essay, 2016).** Stan Grant brings me close to tears (of pride) nearly every time I hear him speak, and his writing is equally as important and powerful. This essay includes a speech Stan made in 2015 in response to the media storm that surrounded Aboriginal AFL star Adam Goodes after he spoke up against racism, and holds up a mirror to Australia and its approach to race today.

- ***Well, I Heard it on the Radio and I Saw it on the Television,* Professor Marcia Langton (Australian Film Commission, 1993).** Marcia is a powerhouse activist and academic. This collection of essays exposes the importance of representation and the ways our media has shaped understandings of Aboriginal people.

WHAT TO WATCH

- ***Black Comedy,* ABC.** Aboriginal people have a unique sense of humour (obviously I think it's the best kind), but I'm confident you'll be feeling the same as me after watching this sketch TV show. Written, directed and performed by black comedians and activists, it's another great example of the importance of representation, and particularly positive representation!

- ***First Australians,* produced by Blackfella Films (SBS, 2008).** Told through the eyes of Aboriginal and Torres Strait Islander people, this documentary series dives in to the history of the continent now known as Australia. From the first point of contact between the colonisers and the Gadigal people of Sydney Cove in 1788, to the ground-breaking 1993 Mabo court decision, this series does a great job at retelling the last few centuries with more truth, justice and focus on Indigenous people than is usually found in mainstream historical accounts.

- *Rabbit Proof Fence*, **directed by Phillip Noyce (2002).** Most people may have seen this film, but it's important to remember that it's based on a true story and the repercussions of it are still being felt today. I watched this shortly after it was released, when I was around seven years old, and for months I was convinced the government was coming to take me.

- *Redfern Now*, **produced by Blackfella Films (ABC, 2012).** This was a landmark TV series for Aboriginal representation, and particularly representation of Aboriginal culture in metro areas. From the first episode, as I watched Leah Purcell drive around 'The Block' in the suburb of Redfern, the Aboriginal heart of Sydney, I saw my own aunties, my own family and my own stories on TV for the first time ever.

- *The Final Quarter*, **directed by Ian Darling (2019) and** *The Australian Dream*, **directed by Daniel Gordon (2019).** *The Australian Dream* continues the conversation raised by Stan Grant in his speech in the opening pages of his Quarterly Essay of the same name, analysing the media and spectators' treatment of Adam Goodes in the final years of his career. *The Final Quarter* similarly paints a picture of the onslaught of racist vitriol faced by Goodes at this time, by presenting the media coverage without other commentary. The two work well together and tell a brutal but honest story of what it means to be black and in the spotlight in Australia today.

- *We Don't Need a Map*, **directed by Warwick Thornton (2017).** Warwick is unafraid and confronting. He's a powerful filmmaker. *Samson and Delilah* is another incredible work of his, but this documentary is really interesting, thought-provoking and a bit funny.

ORGANISATIONS TO NOTE

- **Lifeline:** A national charity providing all Australians experiencing a personal crisis with access to 24-hour crisis support and suicide prevention services. It is committed to empowering Australians to be suicide-safe through connection, compassion and hope. Lifeline's vision is for an Australia free of suicide. The Lifeline Crisis Hotline is 13 11 14, or you can send a text message to 0477 131 114. There's also online chat through www.lifeline.org.au.

- **R U OK?:** The 'Stronger Together' campaign was developed for Aboriginal and Torres Strait Islander people from urban, regional and remote communities across the country. The campaign states, 'Regardless of where we live, or who our mob is, we can all go through tough times, times when we don't feel great about our lives or ourselves. That's why it's important to always be looking out for each other.' Conversation resources can be found at **www.ruok.org.au/how-to-ask** and you can be part of R U OK? Day, a national event on the second Thursday of September.

- **National Aboriginal Community Controlled Health Organisation (NACCHO):** The national leadership body for Aboriginal and Torres Strait Islander health in Australia. NACCHO provides advice and guidance to the Australian government while advocating for community-developed health solutions that contribute to the quality of life and improved health outcomes for Aboriginal and Torres Strait Islander people. Information on current programs can be found at **www.naccho.org.au/programmes** or you can call on (02) 6246 9300.

Who to follow on social media
(aside from @tiddas4tiddas, of course!)

INSTRAGRAM

@ausindigenousfashion: Dedicated to showcasing beautiful art and fashion from Indigenous brands and designers. It also challenges the 'too pretty to be Aboriginal' sentiment with profiles of up-and-coming Indigenous models.

@blakbusiness: Produces educational and comprehensive information around different issues and discussions relating to Aboriginal and Torres Strait Islander people, such as how to write a meaningful Acknowledgement to Country.

@blackfitfitness: This initiative started in a similar way to Tiddas 4 Tiddas, just a young blackfulla with a passion for health and fitness. It showcases inspiring Indigenous perspectives around health and wellbeing (and provides great gym motivation).

@buyindigenous: Showcases different Aboriginal-owned and -run businesses that sell a range of products and services. A great place to find unique and beautiful gifts and artwork, or figure out ways to better support Indigenous small business owners.

@commongroundaustralia: An informative and educational Instagram page about culture, history and lived experiences run by Kaytetye woman Rona Glynn-McDonald.

TWITTER

@indigenousx: This Twitter page feels like the original space for blackfullas on social media. It showcases the words of the most influential and informed Aboriginal leaders and academics in the country, hosted by a different leader every week. It also publishes full articles in partnership with *The Guardian* and on their website.

GLOSSARY

Bala: Brother

Blackfulla/Blackfella/Black: An Aboriginal or Torres Strait Islander person. Each variation means essentially the same thing. But the term 'black' has nothing to do with someone's skin colour, it is more about their connection to culture.

Blak: A term coined by artist Destiny Deacon in 1990, it names the lived experience and identity of Aboriginal and Torres Strait Islander people. Another way of identifying, similar to 'black' or being a 'blackfulla'.

Country: Also referred to as nations, tribes or clans. What country we come from or what country we're on refers to the group associated with a particular land. Australia is a true continent and is made up of more than two hundred and fifty unique countries and language groups.

Deadly: Cool, awesome or really good. Deadly is an adjective used in everyday language to describe something positive.

Dharrawal/Tharrawal, Gamilaroi/Kamilaroi (a note on spelling variations): As Aboriginal languages were never written down, translating names of tribes into English has meant there are variations in their spelling. Each individual tends to have a preference for which spelling they use for their mob, but the way to know if two names are for the same mob is to say them aloud; you'll be able to hear their similarities loud and clear.

Gammon: Joking, mucking around or fake. There are very few words in common among Aboriginal languages, but 'gammon' or 'gammin' almost seems to be universal across our communities. A statement like 'I'm just joking' becomes 'I'm gammon'. But it will also be used to describe someone you don't like or something you think is bad or fake, when someone will say 'they're gammon' or 'that's gammon'.

Jarjum: A Bundjalung word for children or babies. This word is specific to one language group but is used often to talk about children along the east coast of Australia.

Koori: The collective term for Aboriginal people from New South Wales and Victoria.

Mob: Your people. Can be your family, your friends, your tribe or Aboriginal and Torres Strait Islander people in their entirety.

Murri: The collective term for Aboriginal people from Queensland.

Noongar: The collective term for Aboriginal people from south-west Western Australia.

Nunga: The collective term for Aboriginal people from South Australia.

Palawa: The collective term for Aboriginal people from Tasmania.

Yolŋu: The collective term for Aboriginal people from Arnhem Land in the Northern Territory.

REFERENCES

Australian Bureau of Statistics, 'Aboriginal and Torres Strait Islander Population, 2016 Census Data Summary', 2017, abs.gov.au/ausstats/abs@.nsf/Lookup/by%20 Subject/2071.0~2016~Main%20Features~Aboriginal%20 and%20Torres%20Strait%20Islander%20Population%20 Data%20Summary~10

Commonwealth of Australia, 'Accessibility and quality of mental health services in rural and remote Australia', 2018, aph.gov.au/Parliamentary_Business/Committees/Senate/ Community_Affairs/MentalHealthServices/Report

Darian-Smith, Kate, 'Australia Day, Invasion Day, Survival Day: a long history of celebration and contestation', *The Conversation*, **2017,** theconversation.com/australia-day-invasion-day-survival-day-a-long-history-of-celebration-and-contestation-70278

NUNGA
(FROM SA)

BLACKFULLAS

KOORI
(FROM NSW OR VIC)

THEIR COUNTRY
(I.E. WIRADJURI,
GAMILAROI, YORTA
YORTA)

MURRI
(FROM QLD)

WHAT NAMES DO
INDIGENOUS
AUSTRALIANS
CALL THEMSELVES?

ABORIGINAL

PALAWA
(FROM TAS)

TORRES STRAIT
ISLANDER

NOONGAR
(FROM WA)

YOLŋU
(FROM ARNHEM LAND)

INDIGENOUS
FIRST NATIONS

HISTORY OF AUSTRALIA

OVER 60,000 THOUSAND YEARS OF ABORIGINAL AND TORRES STRAIT ISLANDER HISTORY

INDIGENOUS PEOPLE IN THIS TIME BEFORE EUROPEAN SETTLEMENT ARE:

- *The first ever bakers*
- *The first astronomers*
- *Land protectors*
- *Connected to language, culture and tradition*

AND THEY LIVE WITH:

- *No poverty*
- *No drugs or alcohol*
- *No suicide*
- *No intergenerational trauma*

250 YEARS OF EUROPEAN SETTLEMENT ... AND MUCH HAS CHANGED

ABOUT THE AUTHOR

Marlee Silva is a proud Gamilaroi and Dunghutti woman born and raised on Dharrawal country, south of Sydney. Storytelling has always been a big part of Marlee's life. Her mum tells people she stopped reading bedtime stories to Marlee and her sister, Keely, by the time Marlee was five, because she'd started making them up herself. Even when Marlee ran into her kindergarten teacher a few years into university and told them she was studying creative writing, they laughed, 'No way, after all these years you're still telling stories?' It seems this was always meant to be her path.

Her passion for storytelling and pride in her Aboriginality came together in a new and dynamic way in 2018 when she launched an Instagram page dedicated to celebrating Indigenous women and girls, which she called 'Tiddas 4 Tiddas'. The positive stories of success and aspiration the page showcases quickly amassed an online following in the thousands and eventually led to the development of a podcast of the same name. The Tiddas 4 Tiddas community, and the stories of the staunch Aboriginal women in the family with whom she was raised, were the driving inspirations behind Marlee's debut book, *My Tidda, My Sister*.

ABOUT THE ARTIST

Rachael Sarra is an artist and designer whose work is an extension of her being and experiences. As a contemporary Aboriginal artist from Goreng Goreng country, Rachael uses art as a powerful tool in storytelling, to educate and share Aboriginal culture and its evolution. Rachael's work often challenges and explores the themes of society's perception of what Aboriginal art and identity is. Her style is feminine, fun and engaging, yet is strongly drawn from her heritage and her role as an Aboriginal woman in a modern world. Rachael is fuelled by passion to continue exploring her Aboriginality through art and design, with each piece strengthening her identity. Her work has also featured in the Adam Brigg's book *Our Home, Our Heartbeat* (Hardie Grant Egmont) and in other products such as t-shirt and jewellery designs.

Published in 2020 by Hardie Grant Travel, a division of Hardie Grant Publishing

Hardie Grant Travel (Melbourne)
Building 1, 658 Church Street
Richmond, Victoria 3121

Hardie Grant Travel (Sydney)
Level 7, 45 Jones Street
Ultimo, NSW 2007

www.hardiegrant.com/au/travel

A catalogue record for this
book is available from the
National Library of Australia

Hardie Grant acknowledges the Traditional Owners of the country on which we work, the Wurundjeri people of the Kulin nation and the Gadigal people of the Eora nation, and recognises their continuing connection to the land, waters and culture. We pay our respects to their Elders past, present and emerging.

My Tidda, My Sister
ISBN 9781741177114

10 9 8 7 6 5 4 3 2 1

Publisher: Melissa Kayser
Editor: Bridget Caldwell
Editorial assistance: Marg Bowman
Design: Erika Budiman
Prepress: Splitting Image Colour Studio

Background images of brushstrokes and textures are ©iStockphoto.com from binik, Xurzon and hudiemm.
Vector graphic of coffee cups on pages 100–1 is ©iStockphoto.com/Pixsooz.

Printed and bound in China by LEO Paper Products LTD.